The Traveler's Tale

A Contemplative Inquiry into a 1947 Roswell UFO Disclosure

Will Randall

LEAFWATER
Press

ISBN 979-8-9992551-0-5 (paperback)

ISBN 979-8-9992551-2-9 (ebook)

Preface

What began as an intellectual endeavor was always, in fact, a spiritual journey. For most of my life, I had viewed any serious talk of spirituality with deep suspicions, and I'd understand if many readers of this book do too. Yet when I met information that fundamentally challenged the assumptions behind those suspicions, I experienced a tectonic shift. Ultimately, I found a deeper sense of knowing that has a wellspring beyond my mind and that hums within the very core of my being.

This is a book of questions. For several years, I was unsure whether sharing what I had learned was for the best. I struggled with conflicting desires, both wanting to put forth what I felt was incredibly important information and wanting to prevent others from feeling the sense of hopelessness I had first felt as I ruminated on this information. I have since answered this question for myself: Knowledge that may fundamentally alter our understanding of ourselves and of reality itself is not for certain humans to withhold from others. Such withholding of information, such as the form of government secrecy related in the tale that follows, prevents us from individually and collectively facing the hard questions that we must face if we hope to evolve and survive as a species. It is in this spirit that I pass along the hard questions that emerged for me and aided my journey from near hopelessness to something far greater than I had previously hoped for.

This book is a tale of a tale. It begins with what I call the traveler's tale, which in my view stands alone as an immensely important account. With the exception of certain details about the friend who relayed the tale to me, which I have changed to preserve his anonymity, I report the tale exactly as I heard it. This tale prompted me to grapple with questions harder than any I had ever allowed myself to face, and I recount my process because I wished, during those initial years after hearing the tale, that someone had been able to offer their informed, sincere grappling of it with me. My hope is that relating my experience of transformation may genuinely aid others as they embark on their own intellectual, emotional, and spiritual digestion of a tale that points to an entirely new reality.

This is a book about the kind of hope that can withstand the hardest questions. Some of these are timeworn questions about time itself, questions about our ability to steer our own course, questions about our greater purpose. I have no interest in providing dogmatic answers; my interest is in relating my personal pathway, via a long stare into the smallest spaces and greatest things within us, toward sincere and profound hope. In an era of deep climatic, social, and political instabilities, the questions of this book remain relevant no matter the final verdict on the tale and its veracity.

This is a book of choices. Buried deep within the tale is the choice of how to respond to it and the reality it points to, and within that choice resides a foundation for sincere hope. For generations, it seems, we humans have faltered. Yet now, always now and only now, the choice remains. It is a choice about how to shape the future of our lives, the future of our planet, the future of our species, and the future of our consciousness. This choice, in all its sublime beauty, is only a realization away.

The Traveler's Tale

This morning, digging fresh burdock roots from my garden, I watch several sandhill cranes fly overhead on their way south. Their voices resemble what I imagine a pterodactyl would have sounded like as it flew over the shores of the long-gone sea that once covered the land where my high-desert garden now sits. Their call, like the call of deep time itself, stills me. I idly wonder how the cranes, and all migratory animals, follow their course.

I plunge the broadfork into the near frozen soil, uplifting the roots. A waft of earth fills my nose. Most books on traditional herbal medicine will tell you burdock is good for the liver and aids detoxification, and I don't doubt it does. Fewer books will tell you what I learned from an old North Carolina herbalist nearly twenty years ago, just before moving to New Mexico: Burdock is for courage.

More cranes fly overhead and this time the thought deepens. I've heard that some birds have magnets in their brains to help them keep course, but some don't. And some butterflies, like the monarchs, manage to migrate thousands of miles without brains at all. What is their compass? Where does this instinct come from? It comes from the same place, I think, that not only leads humans to move our hand from a hot stove but also leads us to fall effortlessly into rhythm at the sound of music.

A soft breeze rattles the last redbud leaves from a nearby tree before a silence settles. A distant dog barks as a leaf shifts on the soil below. The birds and butterflies seem to be listening to a great song that has been evolving since the Big Bang. They are the song itself. We are also a part of the song but don't seem to realize the rest of the band is waiting for us to tune in and harmonize again.

Such are the early morning thoughts of a man digging for courage on a winter morning in the shadow of a snowless mountain. They are just a few of the thoughts that brew, along with the freshly dug burdock, in the pot on the stove. It's been a long, slow decoction. I raise a warm and steaming mug in celebration of the song.

1

In November 2019, in those delightfully normal few months just before a novel coronavirus transformed the human world, I found myself atop a small, remote mountain, combing through the tailings of an old mine just a few miles from the site where the first atomic bomb had exploded nearly seventy-five years prior. I was with an old friend who was grieving the recent loss of his brother. We scoured the vast piles of translucent purple fluorite, blue-green copper, and jet-black galena beside locked entrances of shadowy mines, and in the broad brown basin far below, near the Trinity site, we could occasionally see barely visible military trucks send trails of dust through the otherwise empty expanse of desert. We scanned the surrounding hills intermittently for the elusive African oryx, which was introduced in the 1970s as an exotic trophy species to inhabit the otherwise uninhabitable military wasteland of fallout and contaminated missile debris. There was a sense of a surreal, beautiful, and brutal magic to it all: the abundant crystals, sparkling in massive piles for acres atop the mountain; the unseen presence of the oryx; the invisible fallout; the stark indifference of the vast and serene desert bathed in the sharp autumn light.

Little did I know, as we hopped in my pick-up toward the end of the day, loaded with a few choice fluorite specimens, and began to crawl down the rocky switchbacks in four-wheel drive en route to

Albuquerque, that the strangeness had only just begun. By the time I arrived at my house two hours later, the world would feel infinitely more mysterious, my understanding of it forever changed.

My friend had brought a bottle of whiskey with him, and he took it out of his bag shortly after we left. He took a pull and placed the bottle between his legs, turned up the music, and looked through the open window at the endless waves of grasses bowing in the desert breeze as we slowly drove along the otherwise empty dirt road. A large hunk of fluorite crystal rested between his feet. His eyes glistened and I didn't have to ask whether it was from the wind in his eyes, the beauty of the sun on the distant rock faces of the San Andres Mountains, or the thoughts of his brother's recent death, which we had hardly talked about but both knew was the real reason we had taken the trip. It was from all of it. And from far more than I knew.

We drove mostly in the quietude of our own thoughts, occasionally breaking our silence with a comment on the vastness of the visible landscape. Then, idly, I asked him about how his work was going.

He works for the US Air Force as a senior historian. I knew he had a high-level security clearance and likely could not talk about much of his work, so I just asked how things were going. He could have simply said, "Fine," and I would have left it at that without a second thought.

But he didn't. Instead, he started talking about the difficulties of his work. He spoke broadly, careful not to go into details. I noticed he still had the bottle between his legs, which made me a little nervous, but I said nothing because I knew he was in pain and because we were so far from civilization. Instead, with my hand on the wheel and my elbow resting on the open window, I looked out over the desert.

We eventually pulled onto the blacktop of the state highway, weaving westward through the rolling arid lands that would take us to the interstate that would take us north to Albuquerque.

"It's hard holding on to all of it," he said.

"What do you mean?" I asked.

He didn't answer for a while, but his brow furrowed. The desert stretched toward the horizon beyond his face.

"You're a historian," he finally said. We had both received PhDs in history and sometimes talked shop. "I get queries from historians and researchers all the time, and I almost always have to turn them away."

I shifted my eyes from the road to his, which were focused ahead. He had piqued my attention. "About what sort of things," I asked.

"Things like right here in your backyard. Things like Roswell," he said.

"Like UFOs?" I asked.

"Yeah."

Then, without another word from me, he explained that he knew of a longtime colleague who had even destroyed documents relating to Roswell because he didn't want his colleagues to have the burden he had had when people requested to see them. This had unnerved and angered my friend. "Destroying archival material is always wrong," he said. "And I told him that when I found out." He took another sip from the bottle of whiskey.

I kept my eyes on the road. He had never really talked about work before. Why, I asked myself in my head, destroy the documents? After a prolonged moment of silence, I let out a little laugh, still looking straight ahead, and told him I was incredibly curious but wouldn't ask him to say anything more.

I knew very little about Roswell. At that moment, we were less than one hundred miles from the small desert city, but I had never been there, nor had I been interested in going. The main thing I knew about Roswell was that it attracted a large crowd of UFO enthusiasts each year to a campy festival filled, I imagined, with people dressed as aliens. Living in New Mexico, it's hard not to notice the alien imagery plastered on souvenir tee shirts, mugs, and craft beer labels. It is hard to take anything so commodified, cheesy, and banal seriously. Plus, I had a friend who had studied the folklore of UFO sightings as an American Studies doctoral student, and I remembered him dismissing the Roswell incident as one of the less interesting of UFO stories. "It was probably just a weather balloon," he had told me one night over beers.

It's not that I had never been open to UFOs, but the quasi-humanoid likeness of the Roswell alien seemed particularly implausible to me. I knew enough about modern physics to know that, given the vastness of the universe and sheer number of likely habitable planets it contains, life elsewhere was extremely probable. But it had always seemed curious to me—why would alien life resemble humans so closely? These versions of aliens seemed like a product of our limited human imagination, and true aliens would much more likely be wholly unlike anything we could have imagined. Also, given the sheer expanse of time in the universe, what were the odds that intelligent life would visit our tiny corner of the universe at the precise moment we were alive? Basically, it seemed far more likely to be a sort of human fantasy—a manifestation of a religious-like human desire to be un-alone in the universe, as my American Studies friend had postulated to me—than anything more real.

"I mean, I obviously don't know," I responded after a pause, looking southward toward the Trinity site. I felt my friend's gaze follow mine. "It seems to me it was just a weather balloon, or whatever."

He let out a scoffing laugh, and I saw him take another sip from the bottle as the creases deepened beside his eyes. He put it down and winced as he swallowed.

"It was definitely not a fucking weather balloon," he said.

My heart rate elevated slightly. I just laughed and looked straight ahead. I wondered if I should ask him to explain but decided against it. Instead, after a moment, I said, "I guess I don't even know the public account of what supposedly happened in Roswell. What is the common knowledge account?"

That's when he started talking, and it took me a moment before I realized what was happening.

2

What he said first was familiar enough. His voice took a slightly more official tone as he spoke, as though he were briefing me as he might do to one of his military colleagues. "In 1947, an aircraft approached from a very high altitude and descended quickly, crashing into a bluff. A farmer who owned the land saw it and went to the scene," he said. "He found four or five individuals. They were short with big heads—all eyes and brains—and very pale, as if they had never seen sunlight. It was like a pale silver. One individual, a male, was injured but survived. The rest died." He paused, and I said nothing. The wheels rumbled beneath us. He continued, "The farmer called the local newspaper, and the Army [the Air Force was created shortly thereafter] soon took over. The craft and individuals were first taken to Kirtland and eventually to Wright-Patterson in Ohio. There, the surviving 'alien' began offering an account through telepathy to a translator."

That was when I realized I was hearing something new—something wholly apart from the official public account.

"Wait ... telepathy?" I said, incredulously.

"Shit," he said, "I can't remember what's classified or not. Maybe I've said too much."

I was too interested to hold back. I told him he didn't have to tell me anything, but I let the silence settle without changing the subject. A tense anticipation grew. After a minute, he took another pull and began to say more. As he spoke, my body became covered with goosebumps like I had never felt before. Over the next sixty or so miles of highway, he slowly told me more.

Here is what I learned: The surviving individual said they were humans from the future—thirty-thousand years in the future. They were not fully organic but had morphed with technology. "It's as though they had morphed with our phones," he said. Their ship was built with materials and elements unknown to Earth, though silica formed a significant component of their bodies and/or technology. They had figured out, through quantum physics, how to somehow bend space-time. Technological developments with tools such as atomic clocks had been very important.

The surviving individual, once he had been transported to Wright-Patterson Air Force Base in Ohio, died within days, but before his death had given a long account of what happens on Earth over the next thirty thousand years. The transcript of this account is what was later destroyed by a government historian, yet there perhaps still exists one copy of the transcript at Wright-Patterson. The wreckage of the craft (and presumably, my friend said, the bodies as well) is also at Wright-Patterson. In the days that followed the crash and the transcription, the decision for the cover-up was ultimately made by the Secretary of Defense. The account of the "alien" had "messed with the heads" of everyone who had witnessed it, from the transcriber to the military psychiatrist to the army workers. In all, about twelve people knew about it at the time. The farmer, as far as my friend knew, had never talked about it since.

In the transcript, the "alien" describes a cyclical future. He explains that things will get worse, then much better, then worse again, then better again. He says that humans will be forced to go to Mars. In those early journeys and efforts to settle Mars, many people will die. There will be significant pain. Humans will eventually go much further. There are many places beyond what we know about, and many other forms of life.

They had come to Roswell, my friend explained, "almost as tourists." More accurately, he said, it was like a mix of tourism and historical documenting. It is common practice, in the far distant future, to look back nostalgically at Earth and at the humans who knew it. They went to Roswell specifically because they were curious about the bomb, which had exploded only two years earlier at the Trinity site, about fifty miles away. It was as though they were curious what life was like just after. Apparently, the lasting effects of the explosion had thrown off their calculations and led to their crash. Even the "aliens" can occasionally mess up their calculations. These trips, my friend said, were fairly routine—this was far from the only visit they have made and that we know about. My friend added parenthetically that the military is well aware that these visits have continued to the present day.

The "alien" spoke through telepathy and had the ability to communicate in any language. The "alien" offered no advice, and only offered a "history" of the future. The "alien" was not without anxiety—worry never seems to go away. He feared his own death, and spoke of a threat from "insectoids"—true aliens—that wanted to kill them for their food and fuel.

There were long pauses as my friend recounted what he knew. The goosebumps didn't go away; my shock was real. I was just beginning to process what he was telling me.

"It has been so long now. How do you tell people now?" he asked after one long pause. My eyes remained focused on the road ahead.

"About fourteen percent of the population would find it interesting," he added, "and about eighty-six percent would be angry."

"Angry? Why?" I asked.

"Because why didn't we say something then? And because, 'Where's Jesus?' for example." After a pause, he added, "But anyway, even if I took it to *The New York Times* tomorrow, who would believe me? I'd just be subjected to character assassination."

My body shook and continued to shake as I drove. After another pause, he added calmly, "The earth will need to take a rest for a few hundred thousand years."

"Nuclear fallout?" I asked quietly.

He nodded. "And there will be some problem with the atmosphere after that. Life will be untenable. That's when they will lift off for Mars." He paused as we looked out over the immensely beautiful landscape, and I could not help but imagine how it would look after the humans had gone. The desert and mountains, I imagined, might look just about the same. "Humans are like a bad lover for the earth," my friend added. "The dinosaurs were good. They lasted millions of years and Earth thrived. Humans are like a quick and bad affair—one that leaves the earth reeling and needing to heal after."

Again, we drove in a long silence. The distant peaks of the Sandias became visible along with, soon after, the skyline of Albuquerque.

He took another pull, sighed, and added, "The fire of life—the flame—doesn't go out. That's the important thing. Humankind, in some form, survives. The good ones prevail. The bad ones, the divisive and hateful ones, lose. But there will be bad times. Forget the nation-state—it is only the briefest of blips. There will be times of division and competing warlords. Violence and chaos. But the people will see through it and defeat them. There will be great triumphs though, too. Triumphs over disease, for example. There will be a series of pandemics, progressively worse, but eventually great medical triumphs will occur. And they spoke of spiritual triumphs, as well. It gets far better, eventually. And the bad ones—the warlords, the hate-mongers and Trump-types—will ultimately lose. It is motivation to raise good children because the world will need them. They will be key to survival."

Soon after, we reached his in-laws' house, where he and his family were staying during his extended work trip. We showed his kids the rocks we had found. They marveled with wide eyes at the kaleidoscopic contours of sparkling stones. He kissed his wife and turned to give me a quick hug and one last knowing glance. Without another word, I drove alone to my house, goosebumps still on my skin.

***

I met up with my friend for coffee a week after our trip, just before he flew back home with his family. As usual, we mostly talked about developments in our lives but, inevitably, the account came up of the traveler from thirty thousand years in the future. At first, I simply wanted to confirm that he hadn't been playing a joke me. His sober eyes locked into mine with a seriousness and tinge of sadness that told me nothing he had relayed to me had been in jest, and he confirmed as much with his words, not only that once but many times since. Once I was thoroughly convinced that he wasn't simply messing with me, I also wanted to learn more details, if possible. I wanted, maybe most of all, to know about how "things get better" after they get worse (i.e., warlords, climate collapse, nuclear apocalypse, widespread deaths on Mars). He had little more to offer, other than that the visitor had reported that things get better on a physical level (eradication of disease) and on a spiritual level.

Sitting over a half-eaten omelet and a third cup of coffee, I pressed him about what types of spiritual achievements the visitor had described, and he added a crucial detail casually, as though he had merely forgotten to mention it earlier. "When the military did the autopsies, they found an anatomy that was more similar to plants than humans."

He paused for a second, taking in my astounded face. "Yeah, where there should have been a liver or kidney or whatever, there were structures more similar to xylem and phloem."

I was silent, taking it in.

"In fact," he continued, "this was a big reason the military decided that they were ultimately fucking with us. That they weren't humans as they said, but some sort of drone or something." He put down his fork and took a sip of coffee.

That was the last time he offered any further information about the topic. "Look," he said as we waited for the bill, "let's not keep talking about this."

I understood that he felt deeply uncomfortable broaching the subject, and perhaps had regretted divulging so much. And that was that. We've kept up over the years but have never again spoken directly of what he told me.

What has remained is largely a matter of digestion, an inquiry into what such a revelatory tale might bring to light.

3

The night after first hearing the traveler's tale, I drew a bath and placed a candle on the side of the tub. Neko Case's "I Wish I Were the Moon" swept over me from the speaker beside the sink. My muscles felt like Jell-O. I had no idea what to think, and I resisted jumping to conclusions. A strange mix of shock and grief, awe and calm flowed through me as I lay submerged in the steaming water, staring at a flickering flame that felt far more relevant than any candle I had ever stared at previously.

To my surprise, the hardest part wasn't the idea of beings like the Roswell traveler existing in the flesh—though I have no idea how I'd react if I ever encountered such a traveler. It was something else entirely. It was the potential loss of hope that loomed as I sat with the suggestion that the future may be fixed, that catastrophe lies ahead, and that there may be little I or anyone else can do about it. Deeper still, it was the recognition, felt in my bones, that something fundamental about my understanding of reality had permanently shifted. This grappling occupied my most serious thoughts. Ultimately it would lead me to a realm of far deeper hope than I had ever previously allowed myself to imagine.

Elisabeth Kübler-Ross's famous stages of grief—denial, anger, bargaining, depression, acceptance—come to mind when I consider the days, months, and years that followed. Grief was itself only a stage in a bigger process, but an important one. The profound tragedy contained in the traveler's tale seemed only to deepen the longer I sat with it. It felt like I was suddenly confronting a terminal diagnosis far worse than the forecast of my own personal death. The prediction was a form of death of the planet I love, the only planet I know, and of many of the animals and plants within it. A death, it seemed, of hope itself. How could I have hope for a future in which my known world would have ceased to exist? Only the flickering of the candle—which I meditated on over the course of many more baths during that time and which became for me the flame of life itself—told me otherwise. I stared deeply into the tragedy of the story, and into the candle's flickering light, as I embarked on a journey that began with denial and then led to an acceptance of the deep, radical nature of reality. This acceptance was built through careful and honest inquiry of the heart and mind. Denial and bargaining, anger and despair coexisted over the course of this journey, appearing and disappearing and reappearing like many branches of a winding delta river that crisscrosses itself before it reaches the sea.

In those initial days of contemplating and trying to process what my friend had told me, I felt the urge to simply not believe him. But I knew in my gut that he was telling me what he believed to be true. He was not the type to cruelly mess with someone's head, and as he'd talked, I could see through his rawness the toll that carrying such information had taken on him. He had no incentive to tell me any of it. And, given his security clearance and the oath that comes with it, he risked more than he had ever meant to by saying something. It seemed it had been a consequence of whiskey, despair from his brother's death, and the toll of quietly holding onto such heavy information alone that had led to the story escaping his mouth.

"I feel like I just showed you my wiener," he had said with a note of shame and shock at one point toward the end of our drive, when the air in the car hung heavy. A bit later he added, "If you ever say anything about this, I will deny everything."

Having ruled out the possibility that my friend had simply been playing a joke on me, I began looking for flaws in the story itself. Does it even make sense? Is it even remotely possible? This was before the US government had begun to normalize UFOs, and I was not well versed in science fiction so had few reference points on UFOs from pop culture. But the more I ruminated on the story, the more seamlessly it seemed to come together. What did I expect would happen in the future? Did I believe that humans would simply stop evolving or that society as I knew it would go on forever, despite all the difficulties we face? That humans would not be forced to adapt—even bioengineer themselves for space travel—in unprecedented ways? If future people traveled back in time, would they not look like evolved humans? And doesn't it make sense to be smaller and lighter for the confines of space travel, to have pale skin in the absence of sunlight, to have unimaginable new technologies, and to have memories of Earth and a nostalgic curiosity for those simpler times? At its heart, wasn't there a *humanity* to the nostalgia of the travelers and their anxiety about dying? Since then, I have dived deeper into these questions and many others, but I offer these questions to give a sense of how denial slowly evolved into something else.

One thing I did not do, for nearly two years after I first heard this story, was read about or watch anything related to UFOs or the paranormal. I did not want to be potentially swayed by such information. Another thing I didn't do was talk about this with anyone. As I went about my life, I ruminated on it in lonely solitude—amazed and shocked and distraught.

While the threads of denial did not disappear, they began to coexist with a new phase: anger. My friend had shifted the burden of his lonely knowledge to me, and for a long while I felt a sharp anger at him for doing so. What am I supposed to do with this? Didn't he realize he had taken away from me the idea of a wide-open future and, with it, hope? I thought, Oh, this is the type of feeling behind the government's decision not to tell people. Because, in the end, we don't want to know the future; we want to believe things might last forever, and that our will is free and our future undetermined.

In time, however, that anger shifted toward what could perhaps be considered a bargaining phase. It centered on what felt like the most glaring and disturbing elements of my friend's story: the implications of time travel for time itself. If someone comes from the future, then the future has already happened. If that is the case, then does anything we do now have the power to alter it? Is there anything we can do to stave off the bad things the visitor claimed will happen—have already happened—in our future? I began a self-guided crash course in physics, the philosophy of time travel, and debates over free will. I was met with paradox and deeper mystery.

There were times when the bargaining phase seemed to hit a dead end, and I faced a wall of depression. I grappled with the fatalistic possibility of a determined future, the prospect of nuclear apocalypse and an ultimately uninhabitable planet, and the suffering that awaits all earthly life, to name just a few things. To accept the foretold future of this tale is to accept a tragedy beyond measure. But acceptance of the travelers' presence, and the tale they told, is not necessarily the same thing as accepting the future they foretold. Amid an ever-deepening sea of questions, what increasingly felt certain is that the travelers were (and thus are) real, that reality is not what it seems, and that we have a choice and have always had a choice.

Accepting the last of these three certainties does not mean avoiding or dismissing the traveler's tale and the future it foretells; rather, it means seriously considering the implications and staring directly at the candle that burns at the heart of the tale. In that light, new mysteries prevail, new hopes materialize, new stories, not yet written, emerge, and new depths of appreciation for the beauty and mystery we embody, made of the same stuff as all else, inspire a rapturous and urgent allegiance to life itself.

I return my gaze to the burdock brewing on the stove. It grew in a small garden, twenty-five feet on each side, bordered by a low, slat fence strong enough to keep the dog out but porous enough to allow the rabbits in. The garden now sleeps in the sharp winter light, covered by the brown stalks of last year's okra and tomato vines and Johnson grass. It waits patiently for a blanket of nourishment from the small mountain of near-finished, near-black compost that lies just west of the garden.

For a little over two years, as I have ruminated on the traveler's tale, I have been tending to that small mountain, feeding it all the scraps of what I've cooked, all the leaves I've raked, all the grass I've mown and collected. It's a consolidation of energy from a global area, banana peels and all, into a pile about five feet wide and four feet tall. It's filled with microbial life that transforms would-be waste to garden gold; it is life-bearing and rich, revealing a cloud of steam and a ripe waft of ammonia each time I use a shovel to turn it over, feeding its ever-denser interior with oxygen and rain-barrel water.

This little mountain helped fill the mug in my hand. I stare into the mug, into the depths of the dark, greenish brown burdock tea that fills it, and watch the steam rise from the rim in all its entropic glory. The mug, a physicist might tell me, is an orderly container of unfolding disorder. Peering into it, as when peering into the mountain of compost beside my garden or gazing at the galactic swirl of the night sky, I see both order and chaos. The longer I stare into order, the more chaos I see, and the more closely I stare into chaos, the more I find order. Order and chaos seem to envelop themselves in ever-smaller, ever-expansive concentric circles. What is at the center?

The earthy umami of the roots coats my mouth as I take a long sip.

4

In the early months of the pandemic, like many people, I took to my garden for refuge. The recent experience of empty grocery shelves and the specter of supply-chain collapse had given many Americans a taste of deep uncertainty for the first time, and had, if only briefly, shaken the normalcy bias that had pervaded much of society. Catharsis and anxiety commingled among many gardeners' rows of homegrown tomatoes, and my garden was no different. Yet the core source of concern I carried with me was not the novel coronavirus. The pandemic added a context of urgency, but at the core of nearly all my thoughts was the traveler's tale.

I had recently moved into a new home with a small garden plot, and I immediately bought some garden gloves and set to work. When I wasn't working, I was either outside in the garden or diving into an ever-growing reading list that suddenly included titles ranging from physics to anthropology, philosophy to folklore, astronomy to theology. I pulled weeds, tweaked the irrigation, put up a new fence to keep out the dog, and planted rows of vegetables. As I worked with my hands in the soil, I examined the traveler's tale from all angles. Like many others, I was searching for an escape to seemingly simpler, more comforting times. Yet what I sought was not simply fresh, virus-free air, nor even the peace of mind gained from growing my own food; it was an escape from the most troubling implications of the traveler's tale.

As I pulled out bindweed and dug out clumps of Johnson grass rhizomes, I ruminated over what I coined the Entertainment Response to the traveler's tale. Art is a powerful means to both see and avoid (and create) reality, and great art can reveal, in ways textbooks never can, the stakes of it all in gut- and marrow-level terms. Yet some art serves primarily as entertainment, and as such its essential function is to distract. Such entertaining distraction—movies or TV series depicting post-apocalyptic worlds, for example—may reflect our collective anxieties while softening them as fiction ("It's only a movie"), indulging those anxieties in the ultimate hope of escaping from them. As we internalize these stories, however, a curious thing occurs: Reality itself is shaped by the stories we tell ourselves. Our stories become, in the words of filmmaker Adam Curtis, hyper-normalized. That is, what we come to consider our norm is, in large part, created by our collective attempts to escape from what may seem to be the insurmountable challenges of our more immediate, unfiltered reality.

Shifting the traveler's tale to the realm of entertainment would be the easiest way to grapple with, but also sidestep and ultimately dismiss, the reality it suggests. It's not hard to imagine, for example, how Hollywood might respond to this tale. Perhaps it's with a drama about the 1947 crash itself, from the perspective of the Roswell rancher and the military personnel who interacted directly with the bodies and the surviving traveler. Or maybe the movie takes place in our present, the early twenty-first century, as a rogue military historian attempts to reveal what has been covered up. Or perhaps the historian reveals his unbearable secret to a friend, who then writes the tale verbatim under the guise of fiction. Perhaps we see that friend dive deep into the archives, attempting to learn as much as possible about the details of the crash.

Perhaps a daring director even tries to tell the story from the traveler's perspective, injecting a sense of humanity in the perceived other and inviting us to relate to the traveler's nostalgic pain for never having been able to know or experience the earthly vibrance we live within now. Maybe that director portrays the traveler's pain of seeing a planet filled with beautiful life that he knows will suffer. Perhaps the director moves us to experience the fear and shock of realizing the spacecraft is crashing, the physical pain of the crash's injuries, the harshness of the sunlight, the fear that unpredictable animals—today's humans—might react violently, and the nervousness of confronting an impending death. Or maybe it's a different story: one where the traveler always knew he would crash and is simply performing the role of a scared and anxious traveler who, feigning a human-like weakness that causes him to reveal too much, dies a death he knew always had to happen.

There are countless ways to frame (and commodify) the tale, but here is the point: It is easier and far more comfortable to look at the traveler's tale as entertainment, fodder for the next Netflix series, then to consider it as reality. It is far easier to simply dismiss the tale because it so closely resembles something we might watch on TV or read in a sci-fi book. We might tell ourselves that we have seen this movie before, or that this is simply a next-level, post-modern meta-art project. We are primed to avoid staring directly at what feels too challenging even when it stares directly at us. We find clever ways to revert to the comforts of believing that it's all just a fiction of some kind.

And so there I was, in the weeds literally and figuratively, unable to relegate the traveler's tale to the realm of entertainment. In the weeks that followed, I searched for firmer, more rigorous ways to avoid the deeply unsettling implications of the tale. As the growing piles of Johnson grass baked in the sun at the garden's edge, thoughts of entertainment gave way to questions about physics. Could I find an escape through science, I wondered? Could the traveler's tale be dismissed by taking a dive into the daunting world of contemporary physics?

5

One day in early autumn of 2020, with social distancing policies still very much intact, I packed my truck for a trip south. I drove from Albuquerque through long stretches of mostly uninhabited desert to the place where, roughly a year or so prior, the world had fundamentally changed for me.

The Hollywood opus *Oppenheimer* was several years from its release, but I had sometimes thought about Robert Oppenheimer, the renowned physicist who led the Manhattan Project, and he crossed my mind often that day. By all accounts, he was an ethically minded, erudite, and brilliant man. He was an avid reader of poetry and had a way with words. He named the remote site in New Mexico where the first atomic bomb was dropped after a line in a John Donne poem that began "Batter my heart, three-personed God." The land sacrificed to the world's greatest horror has ever since been dressed in the language of the sacred: Trinity.

With a few buckets for rocks in the back of my truck, and with my eager and energetic dog in the backseat, I drove into one of the blankest spots on any New Mexico highway map. I bounced my way up the steep and rugged dirt road and parked by the old tailings piles. After combing through the magical debris for several hours, I eventually felt an urge to simply take in the view. I sat on the rocky swales atop the hill dotted with old mine shafts, looking out over the Trinity site, which is itself a mere dot within the expansive White Sands Missile Range. This vast sweep of scenic desert, now contaminated with depleted uranium and fallout, was once home to ranches, and before that had served as a hunting and gathering ground for countless generations of people who predate European contact.

The land spread before me like a bare and textured sea of tans. I knew from my slow drive along the dirt road that hugs this desert that its starkness, as seen from afar and above, belies the cosmos of life it contains. Even now, as a militarized wasteland that from a distance vaguely approximates a view on Mars, it teems with grasses and cacti, insects and rodents, along with the more occasional bird and oryx, all of which would make any homesick human on cold and lifeless Mars quiver with joy.

I sat with the land's life, its silence, its endless beauty, its reverberating wounds. I found it impossible amid that silence not to imagine the moment just before sunrise on July 16, 1945, when a team of physicists, Robert Oppenheimer among them, watched from a nearby bunker as a false sun momentarily blinded the desert, and the earth was irrevocably changed.

"The light of the first flash penetrated and came up from the ground through one's eyeballs," wrote Frank Oppenheimer, Robert's brother, recalling what he witnessed as he lay in the desert next to his brother that summer morning. "When one first looked up, one saw a fireball, and then almost immediately afterwards, this unearthly hovering cloud. It was very bright and very purple." He further described it as "this really brilliant purple cloud, black with radioactive dust, that hung there, and had no feeling of whether it would go up or would drift towards you."

The flash of the bomb still blinds. It still penetrates the eyeballs of those who look closely at this land.

My head felt light—just as it feels light as I write about it now—as I forced myself not to look away from the vision of more flashes to come. Recalling the traveler's report, I allowed myself to imagine the bomb-laden missiles crossing the sky; mushroom clouds rising over cities; panic turned to misery as a nuclear winter sets in; the quick breaths of unimaginable trauma lived by the survivors who will be the last to remember the old world. I thought of the suffering of the plants and the animals who all had nothing to do with it. I thought about the minds of the people who would press the buttons. I thought about how much the survivors would wish they could somehow go back in time and have a do-over. I wondered how long such a wish would last, and how it would evolve, as the memory of Earth got passed down through the generations.

That day in 1945, the local news reported that it had simply been an accidental ammunition explosion. Many had seen the flash and heard the explosion from their homesteads in the area, but it was only later, after Hiroshima had been bombed, that local residents, along with the rest of humanity, learned the truth. The residents, who thereafter suffered from a high incidence of cancer, never forgot; nor did the land.

The man who named the site Trinity was a well-educated, progressive, and well-meaning physics phenom who was ethically aware, socially conscious, and excelled in all the subjects he set his mind to. How do good, brilliant people help create evil things? I twirled my finger in the dirt beside the rock where I sat, waiting for an answer. Oppenheimer lived in an insane society and, conditioned by that society, put his talents toward insane goals—those were the words my finger seemed drawn to write in the earth. Not enough members of his species had evolved beyond thinking such actions were inevitable.

"Now I am become Death, the destroyer of worlds" were the lines from the Bhagavad-Gita that reportedly ran through Oppenheimer's mind as he witnessed the mushroom cloud rising. The bomb changed him, and he spent the years after the war lobbying to avert the development of even-more-powerful thermonuclear bombs, a stance that contributed to the government stripping him of his security clearance, branding him a communist, and effectively ostracizing him from public life. Inner peace seemed to elude him long after the war. "I feel I have blood on my hands," he told President Truman after witnessing the Trinity blast. Years later, the sentiment remained. "The physicists have known sin," he remarked, "and this is a knowledge which they cannot lose."

A breeze picked up. I shifted my position on the boulder and took in my greater surroundings. To the south, less than fifty miles from where I sat, lay the preserved footsteps of a human who walked this earth over twenty thousand years ago. Long buried within the shifting dunes of White Sands and only recently discovered, they are the oldest evidence of human occupancy in the Americas. The footsteps are a testament to the length of human history on this land, a place that has witnessed countless migrations in the millennia since. Behind me, less than one hundred miles to the east, the 1947 Roswell crash site, open to the public since 2018, is visited by a small but persistent trickle of curious tourists, UFO enthusiasts, kitsch collectors, and inquisitive passers-by.

Looking across the land in front of me, I shifted my gaze beyond the Trinity site to the thin strip of low-lying mountains that separate the weapons range from the ranchland farther west. That enormous swath of arid ranchland was dubbed the Jornada del Muerto during the early days of Spanish colonization due to the unfortunate fate of many colonists whose trip up the Camino Real from the interior of

Mexico ended prematurely in this long stretch of desert where the Rio Grande submerges itself below the ground. Today salt cedars and creosote dot the Jornada del Muerto, but archeologists say that wagon tracks from horse-drawn caravans can still be found in the cracked earth. Yet it's a journey along a different axis that more prominently shapes the contemporary landscape: Spaceport America, built not far from those old wagon ruts, takes high-paying tourists on spaceships that take off just a few miles from the Trinity site so that, for a few precious minutes, they can glimpse Earth from space and feel weightlessness.

As I considered this expanse, a tragic sweep of human history unfolded in my mind's eye. I saw in the land the tracks of countless footprints, first buried beneath the tracks of the horses that chased the bison, now all lying beneath the tire tracks of the military Humvees with fifty-caliber guns that now patrol the missile range. Beyond the weapons range, the near-faded wagon ruts of colonists pass beneath the blacktop that carries tourists to a quirky and half-forgotten crash site in Roswell. Raising my eyes to the sky above this land, I imagined space-going tourists crisscrossing their paths across time; one set of tourists leaving behind an all-too-boring Earth to experience the ecstatic sight of space, while another set of tourists, perhaps, leave space behind to experience the wonder of life on Earth. At the center of this geography, this fifty-thousand-year arc of humanity, lies the small dot of Earth where the atomic bomb first went off in 1945.

Wind swept through the silence and I took a long, deep breath. My dog darted into my line of sight. He sniffed and jotted among the piles of mining tailings, crystalline purples and blues and greens resplendent in the winter sun. His tail wagged occasionally as a smell captured his fancy. I called him over. He came reluctantly, and I wrapped my arms around him with a stronger-than-normal hug. He then sat and looked at me inquisitively, confused perhaps at why I'd need a hug in such a fun and beautiful place on such a perfect autumn day.

How could he know that I sometimes consider how dogs, most likely, will not be part of any escape plan to Mars? Nor will the squirrels, songbirds, rice grasses, or most of the rest of what life, at that future point, has survived on Earth. How could he know, as I peer into his innocent, trusting eyes, that we humans—the animals that dogs long ago aligned with, their ostensible best friends and protectors—may destroy his world? I rubbed his furry body another time before he bounded once again among the crystals and grasses.

Such considerations were not contingent on the veracity of the traveler's tale; they were based on the knowledge that the bomb exists, that the atmosphere of our planet suffocates in our own emissions, and that we collectively act without due urgency to address either problem.

The sun reddened along the western mountains as I turned my gaze skyward again before leaving my perch upon the hilltop boulder. The bright glow of Venus began to appear. Astronauts report that when someone views Earth from space for the first time, the most overwhelming emotion is one of grief. Known as the overview effect, it is a bodily and deeply felt understanding of the fragility and preciousness of the earth and all the life it contains. Perhaps a trip to a rocky bluff above the Trinity site is the next best thing. My body shivered as the long shadows gave way to dusk. In the last light of day, surrounded by a horizon far more beautiful than any words can paint, I returned home with a few rocks for the garden, a tired and happy dog, and a battered heart.

6

Time travel had once seemed straightforward and perhaps even irrelevant to me, but now it brimmed with mystery and a sense of magnitude. The rocks from my recent trip to the mines above the Trinity site glistened in the sharp midday light of my autumn garden. I had carefully arranged them along the edge of row cover fabric to protect kale and collards from the freezing temperatures that had crept in. In the spring, I'd move them again to create microclimates in the garden beds, helping smother weeds and trap water for whatever I'd transplant in the spring. The blues and purples of the fluorite, light-sensitive minerals that fade with exposure to sunlight, sparkled in their ephemeral glory. Sometimes, catching a glint of colored light from those rocks, I imagined the intense pressure and fluctuations in temperature that coincided, over the course of eons, in their creation.

Throughout that growing season, the nature of time was often on my mind. It was a cathartic attempt at an intellectual escape from the harder implications of the traveler's tale. Could I simply dismiss the tale, I kept wondering, on the grounds that science precludes it? Answering this question required, for me, a refresher course on Albert Einstein's groundbreaking discoveries about time and an exploration of the work of several theoretical physicists who followed his core contributions with even more astounding discoveries about the building blocks of physical reality.

Forty years before the Trinity test, in 1905, Einstein published the first of two theories on relativity that illustrated that time is relative to movement and space. One person's present is someone else's past or future, depending on whether they are moving toward or away from the other person. While the differences in perception are infinitesimally small here on Earth, this understanding nonetheless points to the underlying nature of time: the past, future, and present all coexist at once. Humans experience time linearly, and we have access to a thin slice of time we know as the present, along with extensive but profoundly incomplete documentation of the past, but our experience of time does not reflect the true nature of time.

Einstein's insight on relativity, and its incompatibility with absolute simultaneity, suggests that our common-sense perception of past and future is not correct. Philosophers and physicists have since proposed many alternative theories, including the block universe theory, alternatively called the Eternalist view, which proposes that we exist in a four-dimensional block of time where all that is past, present, and future has always existed. Imagine this four-dimensional block of time with one end representing a Big Bang and the other a Big Crunch (or perhaps the block goes on infinitely), and we are somewhere towards the end representing the Big Bang. As the theory goes, our experience of the present moment is analogous to a thin slice within this block, and we experience the present moment slice by slice as we move through the block of time, as though each slice were like a frame from a movie reel. Despite our experience of perceiving this block slice by slice, no single slice of time is more real than any other slice in this block of time that always exists in its entirety. This theory resolves the problem of multiple "present moments" described by Einstein's equations; and, with its description of all of time being equally real (and thus potentially accessible), it also helps support the plausibility of time travel.

Even beyond the block universe theory, several key tenets of contemporary science also suggest that time travel is indeed possible. First, Einstein's theories allow for the possibility of time-traveling by traveling near large sources of gravity and back, such as traveling through a wormhole. Additionally, the reality of quantum entanglement, or "spooky action at a distance" in Einstein's words, presents the possibility of teleporting entangled particles, and even bodies or spaceships, instantly between vast distances and thus introduces the possibility of new forms of travel across space and time. And finally, the laws of physics describe an arrow of increased entropy that corresponds to time, but not an arrow of time itself, meaning that the laws of physics do not prevent going back in time.

This possibility of time travel, however, does not mean that altering the past to shape the future makes logical sense. One logical hurdle is the grandfather paradox—that is, if a time traveler from the future went back in time and killed his grandfather before his own birth, how could he exist? Another hurdle is the question of why, if time travel is possible, we haven't seen (or come across historical accounts of) time travelers visiting from the future. To this question, obviously the preceding account provides the simple answer: perhaps we have. To the first question, if spacetime exists as a block universe, then perhaps we find a hint at a solution to the grandfather paradox: Because the past, present, and future have always been happening at once, one cannot kill one's grandfather before one's birth because, simply, that did not happen. Philosophers sometimes illustrate this point by arguing that if someone were to travel back in time to kill their grandfather, their gun would always jam, or some other occurrence would invariably always get in the way of their ability to preclude their own birth. While such solutions may allow for time travel to be logically conceivable, they also raise questions on the most stewed-over subject in the history of western philosophy: free will.

It had seemed obvious to me, prior to grappling with the traveler's tale, that humans have free will. Because we experience the sensation of choice in our lives, we tend to inherently believe that we are the ultimate source of our decisions. But from the standpoint of theoretical physics, as well as in the views of many philosophers, the answer to the age-old question of free will has remained elusive. To this day, most philosophers are so-called compatibilists, meaning they believe a lack of free will at the particle level to be compatible with the sensation of free will at the macro level of human experience.

The modern debate over free will has largely been waged at the particle level. Before the discovery of quantum mechanics, the majority of physicists subscribed to Newtonian principles, according to which every particle in the universe follows the basic law of causation and can ultimately be traced back to the Big Bang. If we reduce our actions, including our thoughts, to their most basic, physical nature—known as reductionism—then each of our decisions is but a link in the immensely complex chain of particle-level reactions that started 13.7 billion years ago in the moment the universe began.

The discovery of quantum mechanics in the first half of the twentieth century changed the conversation. At the heart of quantum mechanics, which describes physical reality at its smallest level, lies uncertainty. Something very strange occurs at this small scale of reality: Particles exist not in a specific position but rather in a cloud of probability—a so-called superposition where they paradoxically seem to exist in many positions and none of those positions at once—and only become fixed in space and time once they are observed. It is thus impossible to predict with certainty where a particle will be at any given time. This is quantum uncertainty, also known as the uncertainty principle. Although it has proven correct in every experiment that has tested it, it continues to elude the comprehension of even the most gifted scientists among us. And this inherent unpredictability of quantum-scale reality has reintroduced the scientific possibility of free will. It has thus kept the debate over free will at least partially open in many contemporary philosophical circles.

The mystery of unpredictability at the heart of quantum mechanics has led many physicists to entertain the famous Everett interpretation. Also known as the many-worlds interpretation, it suggests that each observation of a particle at the quantum level creates a split, a new world. Thus, many worlds spring from common pasts. While current mathematics describes an impossibility of communication between worlds, mathematical models do allow for the possibility of someone from one future world returning to a past that had subsequently yielded many futures and thus many worlds. According to this theory, the history recounted by the traveler in 1947 would represent only one of many possible futures. It could thus serve as a warning and an enlightening source of information but would not represent Earth's, or humanity's, sole destiny.

At first glance, this seemed to me like an elegant solution to the problem of a known (and painful) future. We simply must make sure, I reasoned, that we always remain on the preferable splits as they occur. And, I went further, if we consider that mathematical models predict that split "worlds" would be prevented from communicating or interacting, then we may be able to deduce that as long as we continue to see UFOs similar in nature to the flying saucer–shaped spacecraft of the travelers, we continue to live within the world that will bear their future. Therefore, if we wish to avoid the future described by a traveler from thirty thousand years in the future, we must "split" our future from theirs, which would mean that they could no longer pay us a visit because they would no longer be part of any of our remaining possible futures. But how and when would we be able to know?

Does the many-worlds interpretation provide true hope? The question remains open, but one potential issue for me was that it may allow for the existence of both exquisitely beautiful futures and horrifically tragic ones. How can we find hope in a future that may allow for very deep suffering in some other world? How in one world could we experience true bliss, derived from a love of all others, if we knew that true pain existed for many of those others, and perhaps ourselves, in a parallel world? This apparent paradox left me seeking hope beyond the quest for the best of the hypothetical "many worlds."

For me, the most promising path out of a fated future may be found simply in the fact that, despite more than a century of astonishing advances in physics, much remains unknown. As I write this, my daily news feed reports that Germain Tobar, a physics student at the University of Queensland, has effectively found a mathematical solution that supports the aforementioned philosophical solutions to the grandfather paradox. "The math checks out," his advisor, physicist Fabio Costa, tells the media. "Try as you might to create a paradox, the events will always adjust themselves to avoid any inconsistency." And so there, in real time, lies the possibility that our understanding of the physical world will eventually resolve the paradoxes that plague discussions of time travel and free will. Only time will tell.

One thing has become clear to me: the traveler's tale remains conceivable within our current understanding of science. Disconcertingly, though, my dive into the ongoing ontological conversations at the heart of contemporary physics produced only hints at how to avoid a fatalistic conceptualization of our future. The sense of hope I had set out to recover seemed to recede within the elusive center of the quantum mystery.

7

Winter passed and when early April came, I seeded the garden with a few rows of spring vegetables. It was roughly a year and a half since I'd first heard the traveler's tale; I don't know that I had yet become accustomed to the ongoing reality of the pandemic, but I was grateful for this chance to breathe in the spring air. I opened the gate to the lateral ditch, shovel in hand, and waited for the slowly moving water to irrigate the land for the first time of the year.

I live in a valley with some of the deepest agricultural roots in the United States. It is also one of the driest and most precarious places to farm. Snowmelt from the mountains feeds the rivers that feed the centuries-old, hand-dug irrigation ditches, or acequias, that weave through villages and through the relatively lush corridor that hugs the Rio Grande as it winds through Albuquerque.

As I waited for the water to reach the garden beds, I leaned my elbow on the cracked wooden handle of an old shovel and took off my dirt-caked gloves to wipe the sheen of sweat from my forehead with the back of my hand. The warmth of the sun and the slightness of the breeze lent the afternoon a timeless, dreamlike quality. A clump of slow-moving clouds, backlit against a turquoise sky, evoked a Georgia O'Keeffe painting.

For many years I grew vegetables for market on a large piece of land beside the Chama River, just a few miles south of Abiquiú, and I sometimes toured Georgia O'Keeffe's old adobe house. I admired its extensive gardens, its blend of traditional northern New Mexico adobe construction with 1950s high-modern aesthetics, and its matchless views of the landscape she made famous. But what came to mind that day in my own garden was something that had always been a footnote at the end of the tour: the state-of-art, lead-lined, bespoke bomb shelter she'd had built beside her home and gardens. Windowless and bereft of views, it sits buried in the ground like a silent and dark monument to the pervasive fears of the Atomic Age.

Although I'd visited O'Keeffe's bomb shelter, it was not until I rode out the first year of the pandemic that I gave my attention to the phenomenon of fallout shelters. Still digesting the traveler's tale, I thought about the fear that runs so deep in our bones that we struggle to speak of it even as it manifests on movie screens and in our private and collective escape fantasies. I thought about what drives the US space program to Mars, high-end survivalist bunkers that sell for millions, and billionaires' plans for doomsday getaway plans to their own remote islands. I thought about the fantasy that perhaps, if everything completely falls apart, you and I might be among the few who make it to Mars; that perhaps we might be among the few to survive the long voyage, the minus-two-hundred-degree temperatures, the months-long dust storms, and the radiation of the atmosphere-less planet.

Now, with the strange artifact of O'Keeffe's bomb shelter in mind, I took a long look at my basement-less house. Where would I go if a nuclear blast were coming? How would I live if I happened to survive? How would the vestiges of society rebuild? I shivered, but hardly a breeze was blowing.

I put down my shovel and removed my sunglasses to wipe the sweat from my eyes. Holding my glasses in front of my face, I looked at my reflection. I looked strong but felt fragile. I peered into the eyes of the inner prepper peering out—the one who'd taken comfort from the garden when the pandemic impacted supply chains and grocery store shelves were cleared of staples. I could not fault the desire to prepare for hardship, but when I allowed myself to sit with the fear that fuels it, I asked myself: What is the most important thing to save? Is it yourself? Is it your children? Is it your gene pool? Is it your species? Is it life itself? Is it the goodness that burns within life itself?

The water had begun to make its way into the garden, slowly following the imperceptibly small gradations that led it downward. I dug into the high spots of the aisles, where the water had failed to reach, and transferred the shovel load to a low spot where water had pooled easily. One full shovel at a time, I slowly evened out the aisles so that water spread to all the plants. I watched it move, following the contours of the thirsty land, darkening the soil as it seeped in. I became briefly transfixed by the water's movement, and this simple joy led to a simple desire—to always garden out of love, not out of fear. Perhaps, I theorized, just as gardens can alchemize soil, water, and light into nourishing food, perhaps too they can alchemize fear into something greater and wiser.

Agricultural self-sufficiency, I well knew, is a romantic myth. I knew this from running a farm for many years. I knew it from talking to many other farmers. Even small gardens like mine need, among other things, water, fertile soil, tools, seeds, fencing, labor, and know-how. Most gardeners need some form of help from a water company or association. They need to visit a seed company or tool manufacturer or local feed store. Most importantly, they need a helping hand or consultation with someone who has already learned through experience about the land and its intricacies. Despite the image of the fiercely independent yeoman that our nation holds dear, for a farm or garden to thrive, it takes help.

A honeybee landed on a mustard flower. It remained for a few seconds before flying off with some pollen on its wings. I felt a slight but unmistakable weight in my chest from something that had been growing in me ever deeper since hearing the traveler's tale: We are like bees who have forgotten that the hive is the organism; the planet is the organism; the cosmos is the organism. Bees have no use for a bomb shelter.

The water reached the top of the beds I had planted, and it was around then that I realized that among all the summer crops I had planned to plant once the frost threat subsided, I had almost forgotten one of the dearest. I closed the gate to the lateral, went inside, grabbed my phone and ordered some burdock seeds.

An early summer morning comes to mind as I take another sip from my mug of tea. It was a cool morning, wet with dew. The burdock leaves were no larger than the dandelions. Harvest felt far off.

I had been reading a book on the physics of time the night before. It was one of those mornings when bargaining seemed to fail and a seed of depression felt ready to germinate. Hope remained in superposition. Imagining social collapse, I wondered: How many calories can this little piece of land produce? How long could I survive on those burdock roots anyway?

The questions fell to the garden floor unanswered. A few minutes later, a morning glory flower, unplanted, winding its way along the short fence and framed by shifting shadows in the dappled morning sunlight, caught my eye. I had almost missed it. I had seen it but almost not *noticed* it.

A thought came, and hope felt closer: Perhaps it's not just the smallest things in this world that need an observer to fix them into reality. Perhaps we live in a universe filled with endless beauty, waiting to be observed into existence. Perhaps that is the real harvest.

8

I waited two years to venture into the existing literature on UFOs—or, as they are now called, unidentified anomalous phenomena (UAPs). From the moment that I first heard the traveler's tale, I'd known that I did not want to begin here, teasing apart what many take for conspiracy theory. Now, picking my way through the shadowy landscape of what has long been a taboo and fringe academic subject, I found ever-growing supporting evidence of their existence, dating back to US government reports made even prior to 1947 and up to the recent US government acknowledgment that UFOs can't be ruled out. Anecdotal evidence abounds, and while this is often difficult or impossible to corroborate, several notable exceptions exist.

There is the well-documented phenomenon at the Ariel School outside Ruwa, Zimbabwe, for example. In 1994, roughly sixty elementary-school children between the ages of six and twelve all independently shared nearly identical accounts of witnessing a flying saucer land during a recess period and seeing beings resembling the travelers outside the landed saucer. Several journalists, including from the BBC, documented the accounts, and Harvard psychiatry professor and Pulitzer-prize winning author John Mack visited the students shortly thereafter and concluded that their stories were too consistent to be dismissed.

Even the official account of Roswell is marked with a very high degree of implausible denial from the government. As is by now well-known, when ranch foreman Mac Brazel first reported the wreckage of a flying saucer outside of Roswell on July 5, 1947, the *Roswell Daily Record* reported that a spokesperson for the Roswell Army Air Field had announced that the remains of a "flying disc" had indeed been recovered from the site. Three hours after issuing that press release, however, the Air Field changed its tune, issuing a new press release from Brigadier General Roger Ramey's office that what had been recovered were the remains of a weather balloon.

The initial news report had caused a brief, worldwide media buzz, but this was an era when US citizens held much greater trust in their government than is true today, and the US military's persistent denials of a crashed flying saucer soon led journalists to lose interest. For a few decades, the Roswell crash was nearly entirely forgotten. Then, in the late 1970s, Jesse Marcel, the US Army intelligence officer who had first reported on the scene of the crash, revealed that he had been ordered to collude in a cover-up. He said that the photos released to the press had been staged: Wreckage from the crash was replaced with old weather balloon materials, and he was forced to pose with these materials. He believed the crash was of extraterrestrial origin.

Lieutenant Walter Haut, a retired US Army public information officer who cofounded the International UFO Museum and Research Center in Roswell in the early 1990s, testified in 2002 that he had been taken to a hangar at the Roswell base to view the wreckage of the metallic craft and the recovered remains of child-sized bodies with large heads. In a notarized affidavit released after his death in 2005, Haut said, "I am convinced that what I personally observed was some type of craft and its crew from outer space." Skeptics dismissed the testimony as the words of an old man who had lost his faculties, but witnesses to the testimony, including his daughter and authors Don Schmitt and Thomas Carey (who drafted the affidavit according to Haut's wishes), assuredly claimed Haut had his wits about him to the end.

Meanwhile, in 1994, the US military again changed its official narrative of the Roswell incident, claiming that the recovered debris was not in fact the remains of a weather balloon but rather of a top-secret balloon meant to spy on Soviet nuclear tests. This narrative has since buckled under the pressure of mounting testimonies from those with experience within the government, claiming that the US military has indeed recovered extraterrestrial spacecraft and has been actively working to reverse-engineer spacecraft technology from wreckage gathered from multiple sites over the course of the past century. Also in 1994, former Senator Barry Goldwater, appearing on *Larry King Live*, related a conversation he had had with the late Curtis LeMay, a US Air Force general who served as the air force chief of staff from 1961 to 1965. As senator, Goldwater had served on the Armed Services Committee and the Aeronautical and Space Sciences Committee, and had chaired the Senate Intelligence Committee. He had also been a close friend to William "Butch" Blanchard, who was the commanding officer of the 509th Bomb Group at the Roswell Army Air Field in 1947 when the crash occurred, and Goldwater apparently knew several people with direct knowledge of what had happened at Roswell. Goldwater told King: "I think at Wright-Patterson, if you go into certain places, you'd find out what the Air Force and the government does know about UFOs.... Reportedly, a spaceship landed. It was all hushed up. I called Curtis LeMay and said, 'General, I know we have a room at Wright-Patterson where you put all this secret stuff. Can I go in there?' I've never heard General LeMay get mad, but he got madder than hell at me and said, 'Don't ever ask me that question again!'"

Then, in 1997, retired lieutenant colonel Philip Corso published a book entitled *The Day After Roswell*, claiming that the US government had in fact recovered a crashed alien spacecraft. Former Senator Strom Thurmond, then the chairman of the Armed Services Committee, had initially written a foreword to the book before learning the full extent of the book's claims. When Thurmond subsequently questioned the book's claims, former Apollo 14 astronaut Edgar Mitchell privately wrote to Thurmond supporting Corso and the claims within the book. He included a letter to Thurmond from Whitley Strieber, author of *Communion: A True Story* (a book relating Strieber's direct experiences with beings aboard UFOS that topped the *New York Times* Best Sellers list for six months in 1987), explaining that in 1989, retired brigadier general Arthur Exon had personally confided in him that a "completely unequivocal cover-up" of a recovered spacecraft at Roswell "went from Truman on down." In his letter to Thurmond, Mitchell wrote, "My initial scepticism [sic] of the Corso and Strieber type accounts has slowly turned to amazement as I dug through reams of documents and interviewed military colleagues." He went on to say, "The picture that emerges from the thousands of hours of interviews and data analysis is that there has been a systematic cover-up and denial by government of these matters of vital interest to all of us. Whatever rationale that existed fifty years ago for secrecy and denial has long since evaporated."

In recent years, more testimonies have mounted to support this contention. Former high-ranking military personnel, among others, have reported encountering metals and materials that appear impossible to manufacture using known technologies. Former Director of Science and Technology Development for the US Navy Nat Kobitz affirmed to journalist Ross Coulthart that the "US has been trying to develop recovered alien technology," and that he'd observed an unknown, three- or four-foot-long titanium alloy at Wright-Patterson with a precision weld-type bond that no known industrial process could replicate. In the 2019 book *UFO Secrets—Inside Wright Patterson*, authors Tom Carey and Don Schmitt list several witnesses who claim to know about the Ohio Air Force base's secret, massive underground facilities, which allegedly contain material retrieved from extraterrestrial spacecraft.

Such testimonies only confirmed what I had not been able to outright dismiss since the day I heard that a transcript of the traveler's tale had been held in secret Air Force archives: The government's easy dismissals belied a more complicated picture of the truth. The traveler's tale, along with supporting accounts of the Roswell crash and numerous other UFO sightings around the country and world that describe disc-like spacecraft occupied by small-bodied beings with large heads and large eyes, came as close as could be to verifying the existence of the travelers—not only the individuals of the Roswell crash but the collective group described by the survivor of that crash. What none of this information could corroborate or independently verify, however, was who the travelers of the tale I had heard were and how much of that tale was true.

9

Amid mounting evidence that spans almost a century and many continents, my questions deepened. I began to wonder whether the travelers comprise a single group, whether they exhibit the same diversity of opinion and belief as humans today, whether there are copycat groups among them, and where they fit into a potentially wide and diverse population of extraterrestrial beings. I don't presume to know, but given the pattern of similar encounters (and given how the traveler himself spoke of a collective group), I started using the term *travelers* not only to refer to the individuals of the Roswell crash but also to the wider phenomena of these small-bodied pale beings with large heads and eyes who appear to travel via flying saucer. Increasingly, the more intriguing question for me became not whether I believed *in* them but more simply whether I believed them. While it became harder for me *not* to acknowledge that the travelers likely came to Roswell (and other places), and thus that we are likely not alone, I also had to acknowledge that we cannot know whether to believe the Roswell traveler. And since we cannot know this, I reasoned, we cannot necessarily take the traveler's tale at face value. Perhaps the travelers are tricksters.

Trickster figures, often considered both divine and untrustworthy, have appeared across many cultures and eras with varying motives that range from malevolent to constructive and helpful. There is certainly a cultural precedent for viewing the traveler's messages and prophecies with skepticism, perhaps given to achieve hidden objectives or produce self-interested outcomes. In fact, trickery was apparently the government's verdict after they completed an autopsy and determined the traveler's body to be more plant than human. "The government conclusion was that they could likely be some type of drone," my friend had remarked to me, explaining that as "drones" they were not believed to be telling a truthful story of being evolved humans. Keep in mind, however, that the original autopsy of the traveler's plant-like body occurred a year before James Watson and Francis Crick first discovered DNA and roughly a quarter century before the re-combinant DNA technology necessary for bioengineering would be invented. The idea of bioengineering a human for space travel would have seemed far more far-fetched in 1947 than it might to us today.

Regardless, I had my own questions. Given the travelers' obvious technological superiority, including not only their advancements in space/time travel but also in telepathic communications, could they have been and perhaps still be trying to manipulate us? Is it possible, too, that they are shape-shifters? Perhaps the Roswell traveler understood that to the twentieth-century human mind, presenting themselves as "aliens" and reporting such a compelling story of humanity's future would offer the perfect balance of unbelievable and believable. I considered the example of how, amid a largely forgotten wave of mystery airship sightings in 1896 and 1897, a group of churchgoers in Merkel, Texas, reported an airship resembling a hot-air balloon tethered to the railroad tracks and a small being who climbed down the rope to cut and release the ship and sail away. The event took place in that relatively short period of time when airships were the most accessible way for humans to imagine air flight. Such a story may simply have been a hoax—as most historians, of course, have concluded. But if not—and the suppression of the traveler's tale suggests we shouldn't so easily dismiss such stories as hoaxes—the suggestion that beings can adapt to the limits of our present-day imaginations could mean that the shape-shifting hypothesis isn't out of the question.

But it's not just a question of whether the Roswell travelers, or travelers in general, might be tricksters. It's also one of why they would be. If they are as technologically superior as the Roswell traveler's account suggests, and if they are malevolent, then why not simply physically destroy us? Given that they have evidently decided not to destroy us, we can either take the traveler at face value—that is, accept that the travelers are future human tourists doing research and perhaps trying to non-paradoxically turn the course of human history away from catastrophe—or we can ask whether they want something else from us that the tale doesn't communicate. If they want something else from us, is it for their sake alone, or is it also for our benefit?

This gets to a crucial difference between acknowledging that the travelers might be tricksters and concluding that they are malevolent. Perhaps they are tricksters, but tricksters who have the best interest of humanity in mind. Perhaps, for example, they knew that humans of our era would likely view them with fear and horror; perhaps they suspected that the governments of the world would attempt to discredit them or create such confusion that people would never believe them, and so the travelers held back information for humanity's sake, and for their own sake as well. Perhaps there are other reasons—beyond our knowing—for why it's best to not fully enter our world. Not enough exists from the tale alone, as I heard it, to make a firm conclusion.

While we cannot know from the tale itself whether the travelers have been deceitful, we can reasonably deduce—not only from the reported sequestering of the traveler's tale in secret government archives but also from the accumulating evidence of intentional misinformation—that the US government has been deceitful. The purpose of this deception, it seems, is to instill the very skepticism I relay here. With multiple narratives floating around—some true, some false, some partly true and partly false—it becomes nearly impossible to ascertain which stories are credible and which are purely invented. In the face of such uncertainty, the default becomes to either throw up one's hands or gravitate toward a false narrative. Thus, doubt itself seems to be the point. But knowing that doubt is the point, is it not just as logical to remain skeptical of such doubt as it would be to remain skeptical of the traveler's tale?

The case of Richard Doty is likely just one of many instances of government interference, but perhaps a particularly instructive one. Doty has admitted to knowingly disseminating fabricated documents and false and intentionally misleading information about UFOs while working as a special agent for the Air Force Office of Special Investigations at Kirtland Air Force in Albuquerque. Once we know that this sort of intentional distribution of disinformation to the public has occurred, it becomes almost impossible to know what the government actually knows. Was the information my friend relayed to me itself a plant, designed to be spread? My own sense, knowing the integrity of my friend, his sound judgment as a professional historian, and his academic training assessing sources, is that these documents are real and that his revelation was not premeditated. But I acknowledge that, without a major and systematic full disclosure of all UAP-related material in military archives, I may never know for sure. Regardless, why would the government choose to fabricate a tale full of such dire prophecies?

What seems beyond doubt is that the US government, for whatever reasons, has opted to withhold information at the cost of damaging public trust. To sway public opinion—even among those previously skeptical of any conspiracy theories—the government might now need to pass a higher bar, perhaps presenting corroborating testimony and material evidence from many sources, such as from other governments and from experts beyond the government. Paradoxically, the awareness of this damage to public trust, among those few public officials in the know as well as those who merely suspect some untold truths, may only increase their resistance to admitting to past deceptions or acknowledging what is known.

Regardless of whether the provenance of the traveler's tale is to be trusted or whether the tale itself can be believed, there is a strong likelihood the traveler's tale has existed in military archives. And that alone is enough, for me, to suggest that reality is simply not what we think it is, and that a few people in the government, at least, know this. This inquiry into the tale is thus an exercise in exploring possibilities but also in determining what is beyond doubt: There is something more to reality.

10

I had rarely thought much of it prior to hearing the tale, but afterward, I began to notice every little piece of the kitschy, commodified "alien" tourism that is peppered throughout New Mexico and is especially prevalent in Roswell. Sometimes it felt surreal, sometimes it felt tragically dismissive, and sometimes it simply felt like a beautifully human response to an unintelligible glimpse at something too hard to believe. Always, though, I digested pop culture references to the travelers with deep breaths, aware that the ubiquity of such references only added to the strangeness of it all.

There were a few times during those first two years after hearing the tale when—bizarrely, it seemed—the topic of aliens came up casually in a conversation and someone asked me what I thought. I never knew how to respond; I fumbled through cryptic non-answers, not wanting to lie but also not wanting to reveal that, in fact, I thought about the topic often. It wasn't that I worried that people would think I was crazy or weird; by now it seemed more common to believe in some paranormal phenomena than not to believe in any at all. Rather, I was afraid I would, in my often lonely process of making sense of the traveler's tale, say too much. I was afraid I might start talking about the nature of time and time travel, about nuclear war, about free will, and all of a sudden I'd be met with confused, intrigued faces wondering why I'd taken the light-hearted, almost whimsical question in such a strange direction.

I deeply longed to tell someone, but I also felt a stronger desire not to burden anyone as my friend had burdened me. In those early years, I felt as though I needed to protect those I love from what may be a truth too hard to face. That has, of course, changed. What had then felt like hard truths—potentially *too* hard—now seem like openings to key questions that may be central to the survival of our species. I had feared finding hopelessness in the traveler's tale, yet I've concluded that a genuine confrontation with hopelessness may be essential to humanity's hope for itself. It may be, in fact, the only path, the way through.

There were times, especially during moments when I wished I could just ignore what I had learned, when I imagined the lonely and confusing experiences of the unknowable number of people who have had experiences with travelers over the past several decades. Many have talked about their encounters, but, in all likelihood, many more have not felt comfortable saying anything because of the deep stigma, disbelief, and fear surrounding the topic within our society. Knowing the government may have the traveler's tale tucked away in a military archive, I've often thought: Isn't it long overdue that we, together as a society, allow these Experiencers—as those who have had experiences with unexplained phenomena are sometimes called—the respect, healing support, and voice they have always deserved? Taken together, couldn't the accounts of Experiencers potentially provide invaluable insight into who the travelers are and what they might want? Might there be throughlines within the accounts of Experiencers that point to a coherent message?

One hint of a message that jumped out to me was what seemed to be a call to action related by the children at the Ariel School in Zimbabwe. Some of the children who witnessed the encounter claimed that they received telepathic messages that technology was not good for humanity, that "pollution mustn't be," and that the atmosphere might one day become uninhabitable. Crucially, in the message that something "mustn't be," there seemed to be a message that changing our ways is important. A less explicit message might be read in reports of unexplained aerial phenomena concentrated around nuclear weapons sites. Retired military personnel in the US, Britain, and the former Soviet Union have described several such incidents, including a 1967 incident at the Malmstrom Air Force Base in Montana, where former Air Force captain Robert Salas claimed that UFO sightings corresponded with the unexplained deactivation of the base's nuclear missiles. The question emerges: Is it possible that these were benevolent actions taken by the travelers to stave off nuclear catastrophe? If so, such actions would not only suggest that the travelers have the best of humanity at heart; they would also suggest that this is not a present moment devoid of free will but rather one where the actions taken *matter profoundly*.

Such questions swirled in my mind, leaving firm conclusions hard to find. It's even possible that within the traveler's tale in the Air Force archives, the travelers had related a call to action, and that call simply wasn't conveyed to me. It's possible, too, that, at the time of the 1947 Roswell crash, the travelers' intention was simply to be known and that, had the government responded by being open with the public, a far different course of action would have followed: Humanity would have profoundly understood the peril of nuclear arms before the onslaught of nuclear proliferation that subsequently took place. Perhaps humanity would have changed its course in many ways, and perhaps that was the point of a crash that was always meant to happen.

Young men plant radishes, the saying goes, and old men plant trees. The salt in my beard doesn't lie. I have lost some patience for the fast-growing radishes in favor of planting trees that will likely outlive me. Beside my garden, a still spacious orchard of twig-like trees stands like a monument to times I may never see. My hands placed the bareroot trees in the earth and patted down the freshly dug soil, leaving handprints like unseen placards at the base of each trunk: May these trees live long lives, nourishing and providing joy to children still unborn. Below these unwritten words, the imprints of my knees where I knelt on the earth left another unspoken whisper in the soil: May the world remain habitable throughout these trees' lifetimes and beyond.

How far into the future does my allegiance to life reach? Is there a point at which my sense of responsibility to future life falls away? Do I only feel an allegiance to those alive today? Or do I hold an allegiance to my potential future children and grandchildren, nieces and nephews, as well? Is it seven generations? Is it for all generations, whether they be three thousand years, or thirty thousand years, or thirty billion years away? Any limit seems arbitrary and artificial to me. Perhaps it is simply that an allegiance to life in this moment is the same as an allegiance to all life in all times, as all life—past, present, and future—always and simultaneously lives in this block universe of the eternal present.

I get up from my desk and stretch my legs. I step into the sharp midday light and meander through the young orchard that sleeps within winter's spell. The trees' thin branches bend with life to my touch. The whispers at their roots remain.

11

The traveler's tale is threaded with catastrophe, but there is also an element of the sublime in its portrait of evolution. Taken at face value, this portrait is an oddly *unsurprising* vision of how humans could bioengineer themselves to overcome the limitations of space travel. The tale implies that they become smaller and lighter, and hence more suited for spacecraft. They will become more pale-bodied, with less skin pigmentation—pigmentation having developed as a means of protection from a sun to which they will no longer be exposed. They will continue to lose more hair, develop bigger brains, and lose muscle, as have twenty-first-century humans in contrast to our ape ancestors. The reasons for other physiological changes are less easily deduced. Perhaps, over time, humans will develop larger eyes because seeing in low-light spaces becomes critical in environments without a natural sun.

The most mind-bending, and perhaps most unbelievable, detail of the tale is the claim that humans will co-evolve with plants. The idea of humans morphing with cell phones is easy to conjure, and evolving as cyborgs seems both more familiar and less technically challenging than becoming part plant. Preceding the question of "How?" is "Why?" Perhaps the shift to plant anatomy is more efficient for space travel and/or inhabiting other planets because photosynthesis, even with sparse light, is a more direct source of energy. Perhaps this adaptation is directly linked to the eradication of disease. Alongside these theories are many new questions: How do they walk and move? What does it mean to be human without a liver, or a beating heart? Do they no longer need food or sex—and is that part of the spiritual triumph? And perhaps most basically, are they human?

Regardless of who the travelers are, the exercise in searching for the essence of humanity is a spiritually profound one. I had previously thought that becoming more in touch with my humanity was key to deepening my spirituality, but perhaps it is really about becoming more in touch with the essence of ourselves that transcends humanity.

Evolution is fluid, and notions of humanity, viewed through the lens of deep time, are arbitrary. At what point did a *Homo erectus* mother give birth to a *Homo sapiens* daughter? The process of evolution takes place by degrees over such a long timescale that no such moment can be found. We are always subtly evolving, such that humans in the twenty-first century—the majority of whom have been exposed to the Spanish flu and to minute levels of fallout from nuclear testing, and many of whom have been able to extend their lives with pacemakers, synthetic heart valves, and artificial limbs—are even slightly different from those of a hundred or so years ago. Do these shifts in physical form mean that our great-grandparents were more, or less, human than we are? And at what moment in the future, if our descendants decide to implant ever-more powerful computer chips into their bodies or edit their own DNA, do our future kin cease to be human? Would they ever look in the mirror and not see a human?

To hold on to our current sense of humanity, perhaps, is like being sixteen and holding on to a photo of yourself at that age, believing that the teenage iteration of yourself is your essence and that all subsequent versions of yourself are scary and alien. When I let go of my attachment to a particular definition or conception of *human* and instead embrace the flame of life, I can feel an immense connection not only with far-distant-future descendants, no matter what they may look like, but also with the millions of nonhuman forms of life alive today—many facing extinction and desperately in need of our help.

The traveler's tale not only challenges widely accepted notions of humanity but opens a possibility that we will co-evolve with our descendants across time. It is possible that we are not only a part of their evolution in the sense that we are their ancestors but also in the sense that we are actively interfacing with and shaping their present world and their future, and they ours. Beyond the mind-bending possibilities lies a core-level significance in the tale's suggestion that we matter to the travelers, and perhaps not simply out of nostalgia or curiosity but because the way we live, the future we create, may impact the very nature of their existence. If our actions continue to matter to their evolution, which is also our evolution, then the future may not be as set as the tale at first might make it seem. Perhaps even more than the many-worlds interpretation, then, the traveler's tale supports the existence of free will; and with free will appearing to be intact, so is our ability to stave off the worst catastrophes for ourselves.

I take a long sip and consider how we humans of the twenty-first century are like kids who, rather than work together to find fire extinguishers, squabble over things like clothes and phones in a house on fire. Regardless of the travelers or their tale, nuclear weapons continue to proliferate and the earth's atmosphere approaches tipping points that would, at best, lead to previously unseen levels of human suffering and, at worst, leave us without a habitable planet. If someone were watching us, and wanted to wake us up, how would they do it?

12

It was 2022, and the cool nights of spring had been supplanted by the hot and rainless evenings of what had recently been delineated as a new, fifth season—fire season. The towering smoke clouds of megafires to both the north and south of Albuquerque reddened before twilight, unfurling a radiant swirl of false sunsets along the horizon. The city's acequias, built to flow throughout the summer, had begun to run just intermittently amid early drought restrictions. Two rows of healthy burdock seedlings had germinated only with the aid of some supplemental water from my well. Between them, a row of fast-growing arugula bore the fruits of the already long-gone snowmelt of early spring, filling the space with green. I harvested some arugula for a dinner salad, pausing in the evening heat to examine the fiery sky for any signs of rain.

I considered how as I'd delved into the works of physicists and philosophers, and as I'd toyed with many forms of belief and disbelief, I found that hope was neither denied nor affirmed. Each avenue of thought led to different types of truth, yet together a complete portrait of reality remained unformed, and, with that, hope remained possible but yet unrealized. To find the hope I sought, I would need to stare more directly into the flame.

Whether or not the traveler's tale is true, sitting with its existence had forced a reckoning. What *really* are we hoping for ourselves, collectively, anyway?

I realized that I had never dared to ask this question earnestly. When I look at the news, I commonly see the strongest utterances of hope in the form of the short-term, individual, or tribalistic. A strong rebound in the third quarter; a championship season; a promising cosmetic procedure. Is the ultimate hope that an endlessly stable stock market endlessly leads to job security and increased consumer spending so that we all eventually and endlessly live solid middle-class American dreams? That the Super Bowl will continue forever? Of course not. But even expressions of deeper hopes—for the health of democracy, for the wellbeing of those without homes, for the cure of disease, or for the health of the environment, for example—often feel jaded, qualified, or laced with disbelief, and usually stay focused on relatively near-term goals within society's existing status quo. Deeper hopes still—hopes not just for the survival of humanity itself but also for the species to overcome those obstacles that prevent each member of humanity from thriving—rarely seem to surface.

Is our greatest collective hope that we will finally eliminate all human suffering? Our collective actions seem to mock such a hope. How many people truly believe that this can be achieved through a consumerist ethos that relies, as it has for centuries, on exploitation of the world's poor and methods of production that pollute our skies and seas to the point of our own, possibly imminent, extinction? For those of us who do not: How do we maintain the ability to hope the hope of humanity? And is there any other kind of true hope? Has hope been long dead?

In philosophical debates surrounding hope, few philosophers have concluded that it is anything but delusional, foolish, and unhealthy to hold out hope for material gains. Philosophers across millennia have maintained that individual-oriented hope—the kind that yearns only for more money, more comforts, more longevity—is at best innocuous and at worst a driver of the forces that can lead to individual or collective destruction. However, hope for humanity itself—hope for a sort of spiritual overcoming of selfish hope, of the individual self—has been quite important to philosophers since the days of the ancients.

Bending back to the earth, I worked my way on my hands and knees, carefully weeding out the bindweed, amaranth, and elm sprouts that had sprouted among the burdock plants. I had been reading about the philosophy of hope for months and had traced a thread of collective ambiguity surrounding the virtues of hope. The virtue of hope in many traditions, I had noticed, seemed to revolve around what is being hoped for and whether that hope brings one into the present moment rather than take one out of it.

I'd learned that ancient Greek and Roman philosophers typically expressed ambivalence toward hope, and any positive takes on hope were highly nuanced and qualified. In roughly 700 BCE, the Greek poet Hesiod recounted the story of Pandora's box, a container of curses that, upon the box's opening, escaped into the world, leaving behind only a single item: hope. The story and its translations have left room for varied interpretations, but one widely held view maintains that the one thing remaining in the box was an unequivocal curse: a hope that could never be satisfied. Seven centuries after the writing of Hesiod's poem, the Stoic philosopher Seneca penned an unambiguous critique of hope, explaining that hope is inextricable with fear. "Both belong to a mind in suspense, to a mind in a state of anxiety through looking into the future," he maintained. "Both are mainly due to projecting our thoughts far ahead of us instead of adapting ourselves to the present."

Sometime in the fifth or sixth century BCE, roughly a century and a half after Hesiod, the Buddha, as recorded in the Dhammapada, suggested a similar perspective on hope and fear, articulating that desire for future outcomes makes room for fear. "From craving springs grief, from craving springs fear. For one who is wholly free from craving there is no grief; whence then fear?"

A millennium later, the Christian philosopher Thomas Aquinas distinguished ordinary hope—the itchy and ultimately unfulfillable passion to fulfill one's earthly desires—with a theological or transcendent hope, a virtuous belief that communion with the sacred is possible. In various Western philosophical traditions, this notion of a transcendent, true hope was often reserved for what can be achieved in the present moment. It is a hope of realizing what is, and always has been, possible to realize right now.

Danish theologian and philosopher Soren Kierkegaard expressed this emphasis on the present moment particularly clearly. For Kierkegaard, the only genuine object of true hope is something eternal, for earthly hopes will always let you down. This object of hope, in his view, is a final state of fulfillment that must be arrived at not through shallow optimism but through a serious hope born of hardship and adversity. "To relate oneself expectantly to the possibility of the good is to *hope*, which cannot be any temporal expectancy but is an eternal hope," the philosopher wrote in 1847. He saw the value of hope as directly related to what is being hoped for. As such, he viewed hope based in love, such as hope for others' well-being, as having higher value than hope centered on one's own well-being.

In later generations, even some of the most secular of philosophers have allowed for a hope, built from love, that brings one into the present moment. German philosopher Friedrich Nietzsche, for example, who at one point in his life considered hope to be "the worst of all evils because it prolongs the torments of man," eventually expressed that hope and love were indeed deeply related. "Let your love of life be love for your highest hope," Nietzsche wrote in his later years. If you love life, he seemed to say, you have to have hope; and hope, then, allows you to thrive in the present. Even the quintessential existentialist, Albert Camus, believed in a "strange hope" for the possibilities in the present.

And so, as I ruminated on over two millennia of philosophical thought on the subject of hope, a thread emerged from the writings of the ancients, through medieval Christian thought and the Enlightenment, and into twentieth-century philosophical conversations: A simple hope for material comforts is bound to fail; true hope lies not in the material but in the eternal; and the realization of that hope is found through love, and is always and only to be found *now*.

Hope, then, is fundamentally related to time. Though ostensibly concerned with a future, it leads us, like Einstein's theories of relativity, to the eternal present.

I reach for another sip from my mug and see, for a moment, my father's hands. Season after season of growing food from the soil leaves its marks. When, I wonder, did those creases and wrinkles and sunspots appear? My hand is a clock that does not lie. I raise the mug to my mouth and take a long sip.

My mind shifts to the point where smallest and largest meet. The place where clockwork fails. The timeless place within all clocks.

Quantum physicists tell me that at the smallest scale of things, beyond the point where the most powerful microscopes give way to theory, time disappears. Only when these smallest things come together does time emerge. Time is built from the timeless. The timeless within me is the same timeless within you. We are built from eternity.

13

All this tea necessitates a trip to the loo and there I find myself thumbing through the old copy of the *Tao Te Ching* that rests atop the toilet. I pause upon the sixteenth verse: "To know eternity is enlightenment, to ignore eternity is to invite calamity."

The traveler's tale foretells the calamitous end of a world. It forewarns of social chaos, immense human suffering, a nuclear event, and an atmospheric collapse that amounts to humans murdering much of the life on the planet and leaving Mother Earth reeling and gasping. Yet, in the longer view, the planet continues to spin and, with enough time, the earth will recover and life, perhaps, will return. It is the end of a world, but not the End of the World. It is not the end of time itself.

To many theoretical physicists, the end of time will occur in an inconceivably distant but certain future, in which the universe itself collapses back into itself like a Big Crunch. To many theologians, the end of time is not the physical destruction of time but the transcendence of consciousness beyond time and into the eternal present. In the eternal present, the Big Bang and the Big Crunch have always been existing simultaneously and are themselves part of the space-time that is to be transcended. A realm of consciousness beyond space and time is entered through the Eternal Present, and it is there that we experience the End of Time. According to this theological perspective, the end of the world is not a dreadful event, but the ultimate hope and purpose of human consciousness and all other forms of consciousness.

But why bother to think about what theologians think about the apocalypse anyway? I had not grown up in a particularly religious household and, for a much of my life, theological considerations had felt for me like a step in the wrong direction, like all-too-easy, non-intellectual and flailing attempts to explain a world that science no longer could. And yet, increasingly, the relevance of theological philosophy grew for me. After all, I allowed myself to admit, theologians have grappled with paranormal weirdness, foreknowledge, and the idea of apocalypse for millennia. Besides, why would it make sense to explore the possibility of a reality in which time-traveling, spacefaring, telepathic travelers might exist, but then decide that exploring the possibility that reality might also include spiritual realms—which humans from every culture throughout recorded history have reported as real—as a bridge too far?

I do not take the traveler's tale as proof of the divine; I do, though, take it as strong evidence that our basic understanding of reality is not fully what it seems. And with that, the tale has shaken my faith in modern scientific perspectives that outright dismiss humanity's collective body of theological philosophy, accrued over millennia, as outdated modes of thought and misinformed premodern belief systems. For me, the traveler's tale opened the door to a fresh, clear-eyed consideration of these theologies, an open-minded exploration of what I now realized were troves of centuries of earnest inquiry into the depths of the seemingly unknowable facets of reality that science has yet to fully account for.

As I peered through this slightly opened door, a strange thing happened for me. Rather than finding total dissonance between science and religion, I found distinct and profound notes of resonance. I found pathways, previously obscured to me, that led not further from, but rather closer to, what I had sought in secular thought.

14

W here can free will and hope reside in a theological tradition that foretells the end of the world? As early as the sixth century, Christian thinkers tackled the conundrum of whether individual choices matter in a world where God already knows the future. As philosopher Matthew Dasti writes, "[Roman philosopher] Boethius (and following him, Aquinas) solves the problem of God's foreknowledge by situating God outside time. Our free choices take place within time, as God is outside time, it makes little sense to say that 'Today, God knows what I will do tomorrow.' God's existence cannot be confined to today or tomorrow, and his knowledge is not foreknowledge, but a simultaneous and atemporal immediate awareness of the entirety of reality."

A few centuries later, and roughly 150 years before Aquinas articulated a vision of God outside time as humans perceive it, Anselm of Canterbury articulated what many have called the first Western conceptualization of the eternalist, or block universe, theory. In the widely distributed tract entitled "On the Harmony of Foreknowledge and Predestination and the Grace of God," the Benedictine monk and theologian wrote: "Although nothing is there except what is present, it is not the temporal present, like ours, but rather the eternal, within which all times altogether are contained. If in a certain way the present time contains every place and all the things that are in any place, likewise, every time is encompassed in the eternal present, and everything that is in any time."

This notion of an eternal present has roots in Western philosophy that trace at least as far back as the sixth century BCE, when the Greek philosopher Parmenides argued that existence is eternal and atemporal. In more recent times, a wide range of Western philosophers and theologians have described the epiphany of the eternal present. Enlightenment philosopher Immanuel Kant, for example, wrote, "Time is nothing but the form of inner sense, that is, of the intuition of ourselves, and of our inner state." Kierkegaard maintained, "Where the eternal is concerned there is only one time: the present." And, in 1922, Swiss theologian Karl Barth wrote, "Every moment in time bears within it the unborn secret of revelation."

Perhaps no modern theological philosopher has dived more deeply into the Christian eschaton, or the foretold end of the world, than Nikolai Berdyaev, a Russian thinker writing on the eve of the Russian Revolution. For Berdyaev, the eschaton was not a source of despair but rather the essence of hope. The end of the world is not an absolute end of all things, he asserted, but rather the end of an age. It is a time when humans gain spiritual consciousness, becoming "man-gods." It is the end of time itself; a transition from the world of chronos, or clock-time, to one of kairos, experiential time. "The end of history is denoted by the final victory of meta-history over history," the theologian wrote, "of existential time over historical time." For Berdyaev, the eschaton is an epiphany of the eternal present that transforms humanity into its next evolved stage. It is the blissful end of teleology, the end of progressively moving toward a future end goal in the material world.

Contemporary spiritual leaders have expressed similar messages. Eckhart Tolle, for example, has written: "In the timeless realm where

God dwells, which is also *your* home, the beginning and the end, the Alpha and the Omega, are one, and the essence of everything that ever has been and ever will be is eternally present in an unmanifested state of oneness and perfection—totally beyond anything the human mind can ever imagine or comprehend." Tolle argues that the ultimate goal of all consciousness is a state of union with this perfection, resulting in the eschaton. "Through you, consciousness is awakening out of its dream of identification with form and withdrawing from form. This foreshadows, but is already part of, an event that is probably still in the distant future as far as chronological time is concerned. The event is called—the end of the world."

Transcendent hope is not an easy hope, but it is one born from a deep grappling with the nature of beginnings and endings, and with the nature of time itself. It stands up to some of the harder questions of time that are posed by the traveler's tale. The tale is an opportunity to grapple with a new reality—along with the possibility of deep material loss, which exists as a distinct possibility whether the tale is true or not—and instead refocus on a deeper hope that includes but also transcends material existence. This is the hope of ending human suffering. This is the hope of humanity.

More cranes fly south, and my thoughts follow them for a moment, toward the Rio Grande and its sandy banks lined with red willows and yellow grasses. I land a few miles away, on a campus of contemplatives set among old cottonwoods, where Franciscan priest and writer Richard Rohr has in recent years written about a certain Greek word: *metanoia*.

Metanoia is the first word to leave Jesus's mouth in three of the four gospels in the original Greek of the Bible, and it means to profoundly change one's mind and heart. A metanoia is not a simple change of opinion. It is a core-level change of knowing. It is a call to fundamentally rethink reality. It is a call to realize that thou art that. The most common translation for metanoia used in English bibles—*repent*—falls far short of its true meaning.

Searching for the right words to fill the screen, I return to my immediate surroundings. I sip from the tea now at the midline of my mug. Its color, a rich brown when I first poured it, has become a vibrant emerald. Its earthen flavor lingers on my tongue and in the back of my throat. As I swallow, the tea warms my chest and my stomach. Sun, soil, and water temporarily became a root, and now the root temporarily becomes human body.

I look up from my writing desk, look out the window to my garden, and wonder if I can see myself. I wonder if windows are mirrors. I wonder if words are windows.

The light falls perfectly on the yellow-brown residue of last year's harvest, and a soft breeze shuffles the few leaves that still hang from the nearby trees. Beneath the breeze there is a stillness. In that stillness, deep within my mind, words bow to wonder.

15

I couldn't help but wonder how the travelers might fit into the existing theological narratives of the world. Have they always been with us? And if so, where are they in the existing religious narratives or mythologies? If we allow that the traveler's tale might be true and entertain with any seriousness that it suggests we have lived in a veiled reality—that is, a reality in which significant workings of reality, known to others beyond humanity, remain obscured from our knowing—then what else might be possible beyond the veil?

Such questions for me no longer seemed so easily shaved away by Occam's razor, that old philosophical dictum popularly understood as meaning that the simplest explanation is usually the correct one. Dismissing the presence of the paranormal in religious narratives, from the miraculous recovery of eyesight to spirit beings interacting with living people, had long felt logical to me, but now a newfound curiosity to explore the magical and miraculous took hold. I read the gospels for the first time and found myself wondering: Could the destruction of the atmosphere related in the traveler's tale possibly correlate with what Jesus meant when he said (in the Aramaic Peshitta translation), "The sky will pass away, and the one above it will pass away"? If the tale represents a thinning of the veil, might this thinning be part of what Jesus meant when he said, "All that is veiled will be unveiled"? Is it possible that some of the weirder elements of our ancient stories could be slightly more descriptive of reality than our modern minds had been able to believe?

What I continually found in response to these and other questions is what many theological thinkers before me have found: an essential unknowing. Answers to such questions are a matter of faith, and even faith, at its core, is rooted in unknowing.

And so while I found no answers within the traveler's tale to questions of the paranormal posed within religious narratives, I wondered also about theories that have been put forth in a more secular context. The vast majority of academic historians dismiss out of hand the argument that extraterrestrials or travelers could have constructed the pyramids, for example. The traveler's tale certainly doesn't prove that the travelers helped build the pyramids or anything else of that nature, and yet, there is little question for me that the traveler's tale makes the trained historian's job more difficult. The mere fact that a military historian told me the tale, and that it likely still exists in some secret military archive, leads me to believe that no longer can historians easily dismiss, as many academics have, theories of "ancient aliens." Dismissal in favor of a status quo is easy; grappling with transformative new information is not. Most historians, and academics more broadly, may choose to conveniently ignore the traveler's tale unless it is published by the government itself. At that point, Giorgio de Santillana's pithy approximation of Alexander von Humboldt's famous dictum becomes relevant: "First, people will deny a thing; then they will belittle it; then they will decide that it had been known long ago."

It's hard to blame them. We live in a time rife with conspiracy theories, many of which are so toxic that they seem to be bent on driving our planet towards the forewarned catastrophes of the tale. Many of us have understandably learned to dismiss conspiracy theories due to their inherent danger to sway the opinions of large amounts of people without any evidence behind them. But what happens when a conspiracy theory turns out to be true? With a ground so muddled with untrue conspiracy theories, the actually true ones become incredibly hard to discern and, in turn, believe. It can be far easier to simply deny them than to grapple with their possibilities.

And so I have grappled. I have tried my best, with the information available to me, to avoid both blanket denial and blanket acceptance. In the interest of avoiding any speculation that might muddy the waters, I leave the traveler's tale as I heard it—no more, no less—and refrain from speculation into its potential effect on how we understand our past.

And in my grappling, I finally came to see that I had been reading long spiritual texts not because I was searching for evidence of ancient aliens or historical traces of the travelers, but because something within the collective, coherent message of those texts had begun to deeply resonate with me. The less I could easily dismiss the enigmatic language of ancient spiritual traditions on intellectual grounds, the more I allowed myself to try to actually listen to what was being communicated. I found myself reading passages of spiritual texts with a realization that, *wait, this is true*. With those realizations, I realized that the hope I had been seeking might not be entirely a matter of the mind. The journey that had begun with my looking outward—to humanity and the travelers, to the fate of the world, to the cosmos—suddenly took on a new dimension, looking inward. I found vast depths and unexplored mystery in both directions. And as I went further, it seemed that, paradoxically, both directions were heading to the same place.

16

What began with a question of whether travelers have appeared in religious texts soon gave way to far more expansive questions. What happens when I view the core messages that unify our world's religions in light of living within a veil? What happens when I no longer assume that all religious tales are simply psychological, mythopoetic devices created by anxious human minds to give meaning to a universe otherwise devoid of known life? What if there has always been a message from behind the veil available to us? If we live in a world where telepathy is a real possibility, then does rational thought prevent the possibility that we live in a world where prayers may be heard by those beyond a veil? Have mystical insights and spiritual intuition always been part of a great exchange with what lies behind the veil, an exchange that has, and continues to be, a vital part of human experience? And, finally, what if the narratives of religious traditions from around the globe provide some invaluable remnants of knowing that we can piece together to gain insight into the greater reality we are a part of?

This last question is at the heart of a very old idea that is sometimes known as the perennial philosophy. At its core is a recognition that roughly two and half millennia ago, many spiritual and philosophical traditions began to develop with certain similarities that ran though their essential nature. The throughlines across the many religions form the heart of the perennial philosophy, which has always remained on the periphery of mainstream religious thought but has nonetheless been present in theological circles for centuries.

The term *perennial philosophy* has been used since at least sixteenth-century theologian Agostino Steuco's *De Perenni Philosophia*, but the concept behind the term stretches deep into antiquity, when it was sometimes referred to as an original, universal "wisdom religion." Twentieth-century theologian Bede Griffiths articulated the philosophy this way: "One of the greatest needs of humanity today is to transcend the cultural limitations of the great religions and to find wisdom, a philosophy, which can reconcile their differences and reveal the unity which underlies all their diversities. This has been called the 'perennial philosophy,' the eternal wisdom, which has been revealed in a different way in each religion." For Griffiths, the "eternal religion," or *sanatana dharma*, "is to be found in every religion as its ground or source, but it is beyond all formulation. It is the reality behind all rites, the truth behind all dogmas, the justice behind all laws. But it is also to be found in the heart of every man. It is the law 'written on their hearts.' It is not known by sense or reason but by the experience of the soul in its depths.... It is in this depth that all true religion is to be found."

In 1944, Aldous Huxley ventured to articulate the philosophy in a book of the same name. For Huxley, the end goal of the perennial philosophy is union with the sacred—that is, union with spirit or God or that known by whichever name for God one uses—which is the same as union with the Other. He wrote that the essence of the philosophy can be summed up in three words: that art thou. In *that art thou*, a translation of the ancient Sanskrit *tat tvam asi*, "that" has no qualifier and union with God means union with all of God's creation. It means unconditional love for all creation. All means *all*.

The rest of what lies at the core of much of religion, Huxley reflected, are the various pathways to achieving this realization. Although there are many paths, the paths converge in important ways. For example, practicing charity and unconditional love for strangers or so-called enemies is a message central to the perennial philosophy, one shared as a powerful method of achieving a realization of Oneness. Another common throughline is one of surrender; still others are the power of silence, contemplative prayer, and deep intention.

Here, again, I found myself surprised at the implications of what I'd found. Have all religions, in their core, been telling us that any sense of horror we might ever feel lies only in the ego and the false sense of self it creates? If we are essentially all One, and the way to avoid human suffering is to surrender to that oneness, then it is the ego's resistance to its own death that terrifies. The horror is not the Other; the horror stems only from the egoic self and its illusory perception of the Other as different, not just in form but also in essence.

In the perennial philosophy, it is not a question of surrendering to your foe; it is a matter of surrendering to the same divine essence within your foe that exists in you and all else. In the case of the travelers, then, it is not a matter of "surrendering" to them, but rather of surrendering to God *within* them, just as it is a matter of surrendering to God within our individual self, within all humans, and within all life. It is a matter of surrendering the self to love, in service of divine communion. This does not mean giving up our essence; it means viewing the cosmos, and all within it, as part of the same essence as our own. This has been the goal of all great spiritual traditions.

17

When the rains came that August, the garden flourished. The arugula I had planted between the two rows of burdock had been cut several times and now had gone to seed. I pulled the arugula plants and spread them as a mulch at the base of the burdock plants, whose leaves were now larger than my feet. I felt at the base of a few plants and discovered the roots were as wide as my forefinger. I paused, the knees of my jeans damp in the soil, and listened to my breath, to the wind, to the quiet of the plant itself.

As I read more spiritual texts, I had begun to develop a contemplative practice in the garden. Sometimes I focused on my breath, trying to observe my thoughts and emotions through my deeper, witnessing presence. Sometimes I fixed my attention to a single plant in the garden, imagining that same witnessing presence within the plant. Sometimes I found a stillness in my mind and, from my witnessing presence, which was all of me, I felt familiar feelings of anxiety and fear give way to deep contentment and gratitude.

I still thought of the travelers, and still tried to make sense of it all, but the focus had shifted. The question of how to respond to a new reality had led to a larger question of, simply, how to be. This larger question, I came to see more and more, gets to the core of any response to any reality. It is, in fact, what ultimately shapes reality.

Back at my desk, I pause my typing and the screen goes black. A swirl of steam rises from my mug, and as it disappears into the blank backdrop, I see in it the chaos of the frenzied scratches of chalk of a mathematician's proof across a blackboard. I've often marveled at how math and theoretical physics, to some of those who have dedicated their lives to it, can reveal such profound symmetries and such perfect balance among incomprehensibly vast sets of numerical possibilities, and how their calculations can transform all that once seemed empty—the blackness between the chalk strokes on the board, the darkness between the stars, the spaces between the atoms of our bodies—into spaces filled with mystery. Considering the steam as it scatters in front of my dark screen, I feel as though I perceive some of that mystery—a space where words can no longer easily go, where awe and wonder take over, and where a sense of connection abides. Deeper still, where words fail, eminently present is love.

I used to recoil at the word God, a word that for millennia has been manipulated in service of war and cruelty and hierarchal power structures, but now I see it not as a word for a greybeard in a corner of the sky but as only one in a set of words—God, love, universe, spirit, light, Tao—that all approximate the same inexpressible source of reality.

Perhaps God is simply to be found in all things that are stared into deeply enough. The steam from a compost pile. The most ancient stories we have passed down. The most elegant theorems. The silence within.

Perhaps science can lead to God, and perhaps other ways of knowing can too. Perhaps all paths, in all directions, eventually lead to the same source.

I realize, as I write this, that I know this to be true and am tired of pretending otherwise.

This morning such tiredness gives way to the wakeful energy of letting go, and I allow myself, for now, to take a different path. It is a path of wonder rather than doubt; a path of careful unknowing rather than studied knowing; a path of faith rather than scientific method. It is a path far more ancient than the language I use to describe it. It is a departure from the busy, billboard-clad streets of pop culture, from the steep mountain passes of theoretical physics, from the desert expanses of philosophy, from the hillside meadows of institutional theology. It is a path of water rather than asphalt, dirt, or stone. I find myself no longer resting or backtracking or meandering. I no longer struggle quite as much as I had. I've traded the trail for a river. I am in a canoe, following the water's current, and while there are eddies and rocks and logs to avoid, the water itself knows the way.

My canoe is built from the language of the old stories, whispers of words whose meanings have nearly been lost. It is the language of myth and religion. It is the language churned from the hearts of mystics and passed along by the light of new moon fires and candle-decked altars. It is the language of elders' prayers and children's laughter. It is the language that dares to look beyond the cosmos to the source of being. But language is not the destination, and it is not even the path.

Aboard this canoe, along this winding river, a cliché I hadn't dared believe regains the freshness of truth: The essence of creation is love. And love, at its core, is beauty. So if proof of the divine need be found, it can be found wherever beauty abides. It can be found equally in the most exquisite math and in the most exquisite flower; it can be found in the most common cup of tea. It can be found at the center of the infinitesimal and ever-expanding concentric circles of chaos and order. It can be found at the center of everything, and everything is the center of something.

If the veracity of a story needs to be proven, the ultimate proof, then, is whether a long stare into its darkest depths only increases its beauty. The longer its beauty expands as one peers into it, the closer it approaches an ultimate truth. As John Keats once so radically declared: *Truth is beauty*.

And so where, along this river, ought I steer my paddle to find proof of free will? Where ought I seek the hope I set out for? Perhaps the proof of free will, long denied to philosopher and physicist alike, lies in the realm of the poet. Perhaps hope lies in plain sight, abundant and awaiting manifestation, immediately knowable and always beyond the approximation of words.

And there, written clearly in the spaces between the chalk marks of the blackboard in my mind, I find proof within a proof: Free will exists because it is the most beautiful path to Oneness, and time exists because it is the most beautiful path to eternity.

18

I grieved the loss of my previous, fixed sense of reality, the scaffolding demolished through my grappling with the traveler's tale. But something happened when I accepted that reality is simply far more strange, expansive, and mysterious than I had imagined. As I began to let go, to surrender to *not* knowing and to embracing the mystery, I realized then that I had a compass.

I realized that the language of the ancient philosophers, theologians, and mystics contained far more wisdom than I had imagined. We live with the legacy of many wise humans who had long since let go; their words have always been there to help us navigate, once we individually realize there is a veil that can drop. The north star, they have always been telling us in many languages, is unconditional love, and the compass is your deepest intuition.

With that, a new appreciation set in. The traveler's tale had compelled me to find a deeper hope and an inner compass always calibrated to that hope. It is not a hope based on unknowns, but one rooted in the knowing of myself. As long as we are alive, the ultimate hope—the transcendent hope—remains intact, and its realization is up to each one of us. The traveler's tale stripped the noise and distractions away, and, in the stillness, beneath the superficial hope I had once settled for, I found that which I hadn't even realized I had lost.

I still don't know, after turning it over in my head ten thousand times, what to believe about the traveler's tale. But the process has changed me. It changed my mind about the nature of reality, and with that, it changed my heart. It has led me down a path that has gone beyond the limits of my mind but not beyond the limits of my heart.

It's far harder to relate the inner journey of the heart than it is of the mind. The mind follows its stepping stones, and it arrives when it has incrementally completed the path of its own logic. The heart, however, does not need stepping stones; it simply arrives, completely, when it is ready. What happens when you realize a thing to be true? Words become signposts for meaning, but not the meaning itself. Moving past the signposts to the deeper meaning, the mind struggles but the heart revels. Knowing deepens, even as words falter. It is in this way that we communicate beyond words, trading "I love you" or even the most sublime sonnet for a deep hug or a shared silence that communicates far more than any words could.

So how, in this book of words, do I relate a realization? Do I talk about the moments in the garden when the song of a bird seemed to melt with love through my muscles, and I could not help but sway in a few brief breaths of dance? Do I talk about the glimpses of absolute non-judgment and love I felt toward myself as I stood alone in the rain, watching drops of water sparkle in a sunlit cloudburst above the trees? Do I talk about the deep relief I felt, an almost comical relief, as I shared a sincere laugh with an acquaintance I'd long found annoying? Do I talk about that moment a self-righteous judgment for a climate-change denier gave way to knowing, with deep love, that we are all children, carrying wounds and fears and unknowing, in need of a hug and in search of home? Do I talk about the stillness I observed, the peace beyond and within the stillness, the knowing within the stillness? How do I relate the change of heart? I am not sure whether, before experiencing the slightest glimpses of such love, such peace, such knowing, I would have taken another's word for it. No one can realize something for you. They can only point to what is always and only available now—for you to realize yourself. In a glimpse of this truth, I've reached toward a more sustained, deeper knowing within my heart.

Here, on the outer edges of the known universe within the depths of my heart, I sense that reality at its core is what many seers and sages say is a divine and beautiful play unfolding. It is not a play of tricksters, although they, like all else, play roles within it. It is the drama of the source itself; it is, in the words of the late Swami Muktananda, the play of "self-luminous universal consciousness." It is what Hindus call Lila, the divine game of the source knowing itself more deeply through its own creation; it is the most incomprehensibly beautiful path to Ourself.

The play of Creation—of God, of Source, of Consciousness, of the Unmanifested, of Love—aims to manifest itself through itself. The Source is infinite and eternal, within but also beyond space and time. It is infinitely beautiful and contains infinite ways to express itself—that is, infinite ways to express beauty and love. Our purpose as the created is to co-create that beauty on our path toward the most beautiful possible co-creation: freely chosen Oneness. In this divine game, free will and destiny exist without paradox; our free will exists so that we freely, and most beautifully, choose our destiny.

Life is an opportunity to remember who we are. It is an opportunity to realize our destiny. It is an opportunity to see ourselves within the same timeless eternity that pervades all things. It is an opportunity to see that we are the observers that manifest the world; we are the created and the creators; we are the source and of the source; we are the divine.

All we do and all we experience, even suffering, is in service of choosing the sublime. "It now looks as if something had gone very wrong somewhere along the line of evolution," writes Eckhart Tolle on the experience of suffering and the collective catastrophes we create. "But even this is part of *lila*, the divine game. Finally, the pressure of suffering created by this apparent dysfunction forces consciousness to disidentify from form and awakens it from its dream of form: It regains self-consciousness, but it is at a far deeper level than when it lost it." This, Tolle goes on, is the significance of Jesus's parable of the lost son: We become lost so that our consciousness deepens upon re-finding ourselves.

Conceiving the divine game goes beyond the mind. Superficial duality gives way to formless unity, where the created merges with its source. It dwells in a beautiful paradox of appreciation and letting go. "The ultimate purpose of the world lies not within the world but in transcendence of the world," Tolle further explains. "Just as you would be conscious of space if there were no objects in space, the world is needed for the Unmanifested to be realized. You may have heard the Buddhist saying: 'If there were no illusion, there would be no enlightenment.' It is through the world and ultimately through *you* that the unmanifested knows itself. You are here to enable the divine purpose of the universe to unfold. *That is how important you are!*"

The goal of the divine game is consciousness knowing itself. This is what has been variously called enlightenment, the kingdom of heaven, nirvana, and bliss. "This is the knowledge of the Self, the atman, the true being," writes Bede Griffiths. "It is not a knowledge which can be acquired by reason, or by learning, or even through the scriptures. It is a knowledge which comes from above. The path to it is by *metanoia* ... by a return to the source."

Swami Muktananda explains in his writing that, "all the scriptures declare this same principle: the Absolute is Satchidananda—Being, Consciousness, and Bliss. The world is born from the absolute, is not different from It. All these appearances—'I', 'you', 'this,'—are simply His play." Muktananda explains that the all-powerful, "the performer of an infinity of marvels, becomes the universe and the universal Self as the perceiver and the perceived." Duality is illusion in the play of consciousness.

To see this illusion completely—that is, to return to Source—requires a complete surrender. Deep bliss comes with such surrender, with the acceptance that all creation—in this world and across any other worlds that may exist—has occurred to lead to that moment of bliss. All that has occurred, even all the pain and suffering across time and across worlds, has somehow created that moment of complete surrender, and in that moment, all the pain and suffering is understood as part of the perfection of the grand creation we all co-create. As hope for the future gives way to total acceptance, the hope, paradoxically, becomes realized. From that place of acceptance, from that place free of judgement, where hope abides in a space of knowing, we then see how powerfully we co-create our world and how our choice to shape it, across time and across worlds, remains ever in the present.

This complete surrender is, Griffiths writes, "the difficult crossing, the passage to the other shore, the passing away.... He who will lose his life shall save it. This is the great paradox behind all life. All methods of meditation are intended to lead to this point. The mind must die to itself, to its concepts, its reason. The surface mind must cease its activity, all thought must cease. Then, in its silence, in the stillness, beyond thought, a deeper mind becomes known, the true self begins to emerge. This is *paramatman*, the supreme Self, the light of the Word, shining in the heart. By this light all is enlightened, by this everything is known. This is the end of the journey; beyond this it is impossible to go." The transcendence through the eternal present that has been articulated in philosophies and spiritual traditions across millennia again reverberates in Griffiths's words. "For here the human passes into the divine, the temporal into the eternal, the finite into the infinite. What words can describe this state, what thought penetrate it? It is the ultimate mystery."

In the divine play, form gives way to consciousness. Form is temporary; consciousness eternal. There is no guarantee that any particular forms—the human form included—survive; it is, in fact, the opposite. Yet some forms last eons, while extinctions of other forms occur constantly. The forms that hope to survive must, in the long view, evolve their consciousness; they must, paradoxically and beautifully, let go. And for us, for our species, the long view of our survival is coming into immediate focus. Our choice is whether or not to evolve into a deeper knowing of ourselves. Our choice is whether to know eternity or whether to invite calamity. Our survival is our choice.

19

The first hard frost came and, with it, many of the green leaves of the garden browned. The sage-green leaves of the burdock, now knee-high, remained vibrant and upright. Their roots, now the width of two of my fingers, had grown more than a foot into the earth.

I marked the most robust plants with a stake. These I would not dig this fall and winter but would instead allow to remain in the soil until they went to seed. Theirs would be the seed stock for the next season's planting.

My attention shifted from the ground to the sky as I heard the ancient sound of a sandhill crane, the first of the fall, fly overhead. The song of the season had gained a new voice.

20

Kant may have been right when he argued that the divine cannot be proven by the mind, but perhaps a higher form of proof exists. Its existence is known not through scientific method, but through inner experience. Knowing its existence is knowing yourself. Here, in the realm of immediate knowing, the infinite beauty of the divine is its own proof of existence.

In this realm of knowing, I know we have a choice. We can choose to believe in the existence of our choice or not. We can choose love and beauty or not. We can choose to have faith in a goodness that lies in the center of all things. We can choose to look the other way.

These choices, like all choices, are their own acts of creation born from intention. With every intention, a choice is made; and from the quantum cloud of mere possibility, the stuff of physical reality materializes.

We have made a mess of physical reality over the past several millennia by collectively choosing to look the other way. We have chosen to ignore the sages and elders. We have chosen to ignore the message of *love for all* that permeates the world's spiritual doctrines. We have chosen to ignore that *all* means *all*. We have chosen brief individual gain over the gain of humanity and the planet. We have, in short, chosen the less beautiful way.

We may never know who the travelers are. But we do know that our world is in trouble. Perhaps the biggest blessing we can receive is the one the travelers, regardless of who they are, have already offered: a wake-up call to the staunchest skeptics among us that reality is not what it seems. With that, a metanoia is possible. And only with metanoia can we perhaps avoid coasting toward climate catastrophe, nuclear war, or societal collapse.

We can choose to take the opportunity to stare more deeply into the traveler's tale to the far greater mystery. This is the mystery that has been with us all along, the one in the mug of tea, in a candle's flame, in the elegant equation, and in the child's smile. It is in the eternity inside you now. It is the choice and it is the existence of hope.

I take a final sip and set my empty mug down. I take the decocted roots to the compost. I notice clouds forming on the peak of the mountain that hovers over the city, that feeds the garden, that feeds the river that feeds the cranes, and I hope for snow.

I take in a breath of Earth's perfect sea of air. In this breath, I have traded one form of unknowing for a deeper one. Doubt gives way to awe, fear to wonder. It is an unknowing, I know, in harmony with the cosmic song. The burdock is in my bones. The sun, now painting the mountain pink, will soon slip beyond the western expanse and for now my heart staggers and swells with its beauty.